Mrs Beeton's
Jams and Preserves

Concorde Cookery Books

(cover pic) Apple and cherry preserves (*By courtesy of the Fruit Producers' council*).

(Frontis) Choice preserves with apples (*By courtesy of the Fruit Producers' council*).

Mrs Beeton's Jams and Preserves

Edited by
Maggie Black

WARD LOCK LIMITED · LONDON

ACKNOWLEDGEMENTS

The Publishers and Editor would first like to thank Mrs Mary Norwak for compiling and assembling the material in this book. Their sincere thanks are also due to the Fruit Producers' Council for many of the photographs, notably the frontispiece. Others deserving of thanks are: the Australian Recipe Service; the British Farm Produce Council; the various other institutions which have given specialist help and advice.

© Ward Lock Limited 1974

Paperbound ISBN o 7063 1882 X
Casebound ISBN o 7063 1881 1

First published in Great Britain in 1974 by Ward Lock Limited, 116 Baker Street, London, W1M 2BB

Designed by Kaye Bellman

Text filmset in Baskerville

Made and Printed in Great Britain by Cox & Wyman Ltd., London, Fakenham and Reading

Contents

Weights and Measures Used in this Book.

Liquid measures

60 drops	1 teaspoon
3 teaspoons	1 tablespoon
4 tablespoons	$\frac{1}{2}$ gill
1 gill	$\frac{1}{4}$ pint
4 gills	1 pint
2 pints	1 quart
4 quarts	1 gallon

Homely solid measures

The spoons are British Standard teaspoons and tablespoons, which hold the amounts of liquid given above. They are measured with the contents levelled off, i.e. all the spoonfuls are level spoonfuls.

The cup is a British Standard measuring cup which holds 10 fluid oz or an Imperial $\frac{1}{2}$ pint.

Flour, sifted	3 tablespoons	1 oz
Castor or granulated sugar	2 tablespoons	$1\frac{1}{4}$ oz
Icing sugar, sifted	3 tablespoons	1 oz
Butter or margarine	2 tablespoons	$1\frac{1}{4}$ oz
Cornflour	2 tablespoons	1 oz
Granulated or powdered gelatine	4 teaspoons	$\frac{1}{2}$ oz
Golden syrup or treacle	1 tablespoon	1 oz
Flour, sifted	1 cup	5 oz
Castor or granulated sugar	1 cup	9 oz
Icing sugar, sifted	1 cup	5 oz
Butter or margarine	1 cup	9 oz
Cornflour	1 cup	8 oz
Golden syrup or treacle	1 cup	1 lb

Note: To measure pints, quarts or gallons of whole fruit, fill a pint or 2-pint pudding basin or measuring jug; 4 2-pint jugs, filled level with the brim, give 1 gallon fruit.

Metric measures

Precise metric equivalents are not very useful. The weights are almost impossible to measure accurately, and are not used in ordinary cooking. Schools use a 25-gram unit for re-tested recipes. This means that they can use existing equipment. For instance, a 6-inch sandwich tin can be used for a 15-cm one, and a 7-inch tin for an 18-cm one. Yorkshire pudding using 100 grams plain flour fits into a 20×14 cm $(8 \times 5\frac{1}{2}$ in$)$ baking tin. Mrs Beeton's recipes are all being re-tested so that they can be converted to metric measures when these come into general use.

Oven temperatures

	Electric	Celsius	Gas
Very cool	225 °F	110 °C	$\frac{1}{4}$
Very cool	250 °F	130 °C	$\frac{1}{2}$
Very cool	275 °F	140 °C	1
Cool	300 °F	150 °C	2
Warm	325 °F	170 °C	3
Moderate	350 °F	180 °C	4
Fairly hot	375 °F	190 °C	5
Fairly hot	400 °F	200 °C	6
Hot	425 °F	220 °C	7
Very hot	450 °F	230 °C	8
Very hot	475 °F	240 °C	9

The different degrees to which sugar is boiled are classed as follows:

Sugar boiling temperatures

1 Small Thread	102 °C, 215 °F
2 Large Thread	103 °C, 217 °F
3 Small Pearl	104 °C, 220 °F
4 Large Pearl	106 °C, 222 °F
5 Small Blow	110 °C, 230 °F
6 Large Blow or Feather	112 °C, 233 °F
7 Small Ball	114 °C, 237 °F
8 Large Ball	119 °C, 247 °F
9 Small Crack	143 °C, 290 °F
10 Large Crack	154 °C, 310 °F
11 Caramel	177 °C, 350 °F

Setting points

The setting point for jams, jellies and similar preserves, and for chutneys and pickles, is usually 104 °C (220 °F). But occasionally 104–106 °C (220–222 °F) gives a better set. It depends on the amount of sugar and acid in the preserve.

Note: A good recipe should give a yield of 5 lb jam for every 3 lb sugar used. But fruit varies in quality, and the type of pan you use affects its cooking too. So the same jam or jelly recipe may give slightly different yields from household to household.

Deep fat frying table

Food	Bread Browns In	Fat Temp	Oil Temp
Uncooked mixtures, e.g. doughnuts	1 minute	370–375 °F	375–385 °F
Cooked mixtures, e.g. fish cakes	40 seconds	380–385 °F	385 °F

Introduction

THE OLD ART of preserving wild and garden produce is being revived joyfully today, by housewives who want to balance their budgets by saving cheap and fresh foods for the leafless, dark days of winter. Preserving fresh produce was vital in the past when people's only source of food was the local countryside. They dared not waste a scrap of summer's bounty; for lean months were coming when the food would be scarce and boring in its sameness.

Home freezing is the newest type of preserving; and it has encouraged many people to increase the size of their vegetable gardens, to plant fruit trees and herb borders, and to look more closely at seasonal gluts of market produce, and at the hedgerow harvest. The result has been a stimulus to other forms of preserving, so that home wine-making is becoming ever more popular, and the making of jams, jellies, marmalades and spicy pickles is undergoing a revival; they are both healthy and well-flavoured. Many people, too, enjoy making food delicacies to give as presents, putting their craft instead of money into these gifts. So the more specialized tasks of preserving in wines and spirits, of making syrups and of candying fruit and flowers are also being studied. The end products are often not only cheaper but more unusual than modern commercial products. In this book there are recipes both old and new; but the methods have been adapted to today's equipment so that housewives will enjoy the best of both worlds, preparing delicious preserves quickly and efficiently.

Jam-Making is Easy

JAMS IN GENERAL

The fruits from which jams and jellies are made contain different amounts of sugar, acid and pectin (a natural gum-like substance). All three are essential to the 'set' of a jam or jelly, and fruits can be divided into:

1 Fruits which make a well-set jam or jelly, e.g. apples, blackcurrants, damsons, gooseberries, plums and redcurrants.

2 Berries of medium-setting quality, e.g. apricots, blackberries, raspberries and loganberries.

3 Fruits which set poorly, e.g. cherries, strawberries.

If you are doubtful about the pectin content of a crop of fruit, use the Pectin Test below. But in all recipes in this book, pectin is already added to medium- and poor-setting fruits, either by adding pectin-rich fruit (as in blackberry and apple jam) or juice (e.g. lemon juice) or commercial pectin (such as is found in whole strawberry jam).

Choice of fruits for jams and jellies

Choose firm ripe fruit, or just ripe and under-ripe fruit. Over-ripe fruit will not set as jam. (Gooseberries must be under-ripe and hard.)

Choice of preserving pan for jams

Choose a pan which is large enough. It should not be more than half full when the fruit and sugar are in because they must boil together rapidly without risk of boiling over. A pressure cooker

(Left) Plate test for setting of jam   (Right) Flake test for setting jam.

must never be more than half filled when ready for pressure-cooking jams.

Use a preserving pan, or a large pan of aluminium, stainless steel or unchipped enamel (it should be unchipped, otherwise the jam may stick and burn, or the iron may spoil its colour). Copper or brass preserving pans can be used as long as any metal polish used for cleaning is thoroughly removed; but jam made in these pans may contain less vitamin C. Do not use iron or zinc pans. The fruit acid will attack the metal, and the colour and flavour of the jam will be spoiled.

To prevent jam sticking and to help avoid scum, rub the inside of any pan with glycerine or a small piece of butter or margarine before use.

Testing for setting point

There are several tests for setting point including the simple methods given below. Unless you are told otherwise in a recipe, jams are usually tested when high frothing ceases and the boiling becomes noisy, with heavy plopping bubbles. If the jam is not set then continue testing frequently until it does.

1 Cold plate test Remove the pan from the heat (otherwise setting point may be missed while this test is being made). Spoon a little jam on to a cold plate or saucer, and allow it to cool. If setting point has been reached, the surface will set firm and will wrinkle when pushed with the finger.

2 Temperature test For this you need an accurate thermometer in degrees up to and above 104 °C (220 °F). Put the thermometer in hot water before (and after) use. Stir the jam thoroughly so that it is an even temperature throughout. Insert the thermometer, holding it well in. Provided you use a reliable recipe which gives sufficient acid and sugar, you should obtain a good set at 104 °C (220 °F). Use this test in conjunction with the Flake Test.

3 Flake test Dip a clean wooden spoon into the jam, remove it and twirl it around until the jam on it has cooled slightly. Then tilt the spoon to allow the jam to drop from it; if it has been boiled sufficiently, the jam will partially set on the spoon and the drops will run together to form flakes which will fall cleanly and sharply.

4 Volume test In a good recipe you should get 5 lb of jam for every 3 lb of sugar used.

To test the volume of the jam:
(a) Before making the jam, fill a 1 lb jam jar with water and pour the water into the preserving pan. See that the pan is perfectly level. Repeat this process for as many pounds of jam as you intend to make.
(b) hold the handle of a wooden spoon upright in the centre of the pan, and mark on it the level of the water. Then empty the pan and make the jam.
(c) when the jam is to be tested remove it from the heat so that the bubbling will subside, then hold upright in it the handle of the wooden spoon.

A good-setting jam should be obtained when the level has been boiled down to the mark on the spoon handle.
It is an excellent plan to have another wooden spoon marked off in this way permanently, to give the level in the centre of your pan for each pint of liquid it contains. Then, if a recipe calls for the addition of 1 lb sugar to every 1 pint jam or marmalade, you can easily measure how many

pints the pan contains. Use a pint measure in place of the jam jar, to pour the water in.

Test for pectin

When the fruit has cooked till tender, squeeze out a teasp of juice. Place to cool in a cup or glass. Then add 3 teasp methylated spirits. Shake gently and leave 1 min. If there is plenty of pectin in the fruit, a transparent jelly-like lump will form. If there is only a moderate amount of pectin, there may be two or three lumps, not very firm. If there is insufficient pectin, the lump will break into many small pieces and the fruit should be simmered for a little longer before a further pectin test is made. It is a waste of effort to attempt to make jam or jelly if there is only a poor amount of pectin. It is wiser to mix the fruit with another which is known to be a good setter, e.g. apple.

APPLE GINGER JAM

3 lb apples	Juice of 1 lemon
1 oz bruised root ginger	3 lb sugar
1 pt water	4 oz crystallized ginger

Peel, core and cut up the apples, tying the peel, cores and bruised root ginger in muslin. Place the apples, water and bag of peel in the preserving-pan with the lemon juice and cook slowly until tender. Remove the bag of peel after squeezing. Add the sugar, and the crystallized ginger cut into neat pieces. Allow the sugar to dissolve over a low heat and then boil rapidly until setting point is reached. Pot and cover immediately.

Yield—approx 5 lb

APPLE, PEAR AND PLUM JAM

1½ lb cooking apples	1½ lb plums
1½ lb ripe pears	3¾ lb sugar
	½ oz root ginger

Peel and core the apples and pears. Skin the plums and remove their stones. Put all the fruit into a pan, and add the bruised root ginger tied into a muslin bag. Simmer until the fruit is soft but not broken. Also, a little water may be added to prevent burning if necessary. Stir in the sugar until it has dissolved, and then boil hard to setting point. Take out the bag of ginger, and pour the jam into hot jars.

Yield—6–7 lb

APRICOT JAM (Fresh Fruit)

3 lb fresh apricots	3 lb sugar
½ pt water	

Wash, halve and stone the fruit and put into the preserving-pan with the water. If desired, crack a few of the stones, remove the kernels and blanch them by dipping in boiling water. Add the halved kernels to the pan. Simmer till tender and the contents of the pan are reduced. Add the sugar and stir over a low heat till dissolved. Bring to the boil and boil rapidly until setting point is reached. Skim, pot and cover.

Yield—5 lb

APRICOT JAM
(Fresh Fruit with added pectin)

2 lb ripe apricots	3 lb sugar
¼ pt water	½ bottle pectin
3 tablsp lemon juice	

Use only ripe fruit. Wash, stone and cut the apricots into slices. Do not peel. Place the fruit in a preserving pan with the water and lemon juice. Cover and simmer for 20 min until the fruit is tender. Add the sugar, stir over a low heat until it has dissolved. Bring to a rolling boil and boil rapidly for 1 min, stirring occasionally. Remove from the heat. Stir in the pectin. Cool 5 min. Pot and put on waxed discs immediately. Cover and label.
A few blanched kernels may be added to the fruit.

Yield—5 lb

APRICOT or PEACH JAM
(Dried Fruit)

This is a popular jam for making in the winter when most other fruits are scarce.

1 lb dried apricots	3 lb sugar
OR peaches	2–3 oz blanched
2–3 pt water (2 pt	and finely
for peaches, 3 pt	shredded
for apricots)	almonds
Juice of 1 lemon	(optional)

Wash the fruit and put in a basin with the water. Soak for 24–48 hr. Transfer the fruit and water to the preserving pan and simmer for 30 min, stirring occasionally. Add the sugar, lemon juice and the shredded almonds. Stir over a low heat until the sugar is dissolved. Boil rapidly until setting point is reached. Skim, pot and cover.

Yield—approx 5 lb

BLACKBERRY JAM

3 lb blackberries	3 lb sugar
2 tablesp lemon juice	

Pick over the blackberries, wash gently but thoroughly. Place the berries in the pan with the lemon juice and simmer gently until the fruit is cooked and well softened. Add the sugar and stir over a low heat till dissolved. Bring to the boil and boil rapidly until setting point is reached. Skim. Pour into hot, dry jars. Cover.

Yield—5 lb

BLACKBERRY AND APPLE JAM

¾ lb sour apples	½ pt water
(weighed when	2 lb blackberries
peeled and cored)	3 lb sugar

Slice the apples and stew them till soft in ¼ pt of the water. Pick over the blackberries, add the other ¼ pt of water and stew slowly in another pan till tender. Mix the 2 cooked fruits together. Add the sugar, heat gently until dissolved, then boil rapidly until setting point is reached. Skim, pour into warm, dry jars and cover.

Yield—5 lb

BLACKCURRANT JAM

2 lb blackcurrants	3 lb sugar
1½ pt water	

Remove currants from the stalks. If the fruit is dirty, wash it thoroughly and drain. Put into the preserving pan with the water, and stew slowly till the skins are soft. This will take at least ½ hr, probably more. As the pulp thickens, stir frequently to prevent burning. Add the sugar, stir over a low heat until dissolved, then boil rapidly till setting point is reached. (Test for set at intervals after about 10 min rapid boiling.) Skim, pour into dry, warm jars and cover.
Note: This is a good jam for beginners—it sets very easily. But beware of adding the sugar too soon, otherwise hard, 'boot-button' currants will result.

Yield—5 lb

Blackcurrant jam makes this Pavlova dessert delicious. Candied angelica adds a fresh colour touch.

CHERRY (BLACK) JAM (with added pectin)

$2\frac{1}{2}$ lb black cherries
   (after stoning)
$\frac{1}{4}$ pt water
6 tablesp lemon
   juice
3 lb sugar
1 bottle pectin

Place the washed and stoned cherries in a preserving pan with the water and lemon juice. Cook gently with the lid on for 15 min. Remove lid. Add the sugar and stir over gentle heat until it has dissolved. Bring to a full rolling boil and boil rapidly for 3 min. Remove from the heat, stir in the pectin, return to the heat, bring to the boil and boil for 1 min only. Cool for 15 min to prevent fruit rising. Pot and put on waxed discs immediately. Cover and label.

Yield—5 lb

CHERRY (MORELLO) JAM (with added pectin)

$2\frac{1}{2}$ lb Morello
   cherries (after
   stoning)
$\frac{1}{4}$ pt water
3 tablesp lemon
   juice
3 lb sugar
1 bottle pectin

Place the washed and stoned cherries in a preserving pan with the water and lemon juice. Simmer with the lid on for 15 min. Remove lid. Add the sugar and stir over a low heat until it has dissolved. Bring to a rolling boil and boil rapidly for 3 min. Remove from heat, add the pectin and stir well. Cool for 15 min. Pot and put on waxed discs immediately. Cover and label when cold.

Yield—5 lb

CHERRY AND GOOSEBERRY JAM

3 lb Morello cherries
1½ lb red gooseberries
¼ oz tartaric acid
4 lb sugar

Remove the stones from the cherries. Top and tail the gooseberries. Put the cherries and gooseberries into a pan and heat gently until the juice flows. Add the acid and simmer until the fruit is soft. Stir in the sugar until it has dissolved, and then boil hard to setting point. Pour into hot jars.

Yield—6–7 lb

DAMSON JAM

2½ lb damsons   **3 lb sugar**
¾–1 pt water

Remove the stalks, wash the damsons and put into the pan with the water. Stew slowly until the damsons are well broken down. Add the sugar, stir over a low heat till dissolved, bring to the boil, then boil rapidly. Remove the stones as they rise to the surface (a stone-basket clipped to the side of the pan is useful for holding the stones, and allows any liquid to drip back into the pan). (Test for set after about 10 min boiling.) Continue boiling rapidly until setting point is reached. Skim, pour into dry, warm jars and cover.

Yield—5 lb

GOOSEBERRY JAM— GREEN OR RED

2¼ lb gooseberries   **3 lb sugar**
¾–1 pt water

Pick or buy the gooseberries while still green. Top and tail and wash them, and put in a pan with the water. Simmer gently until the fruit is soft; this may take ½ hr or longer. Then add the sugar and stir over a low heat until dissolved. Bring to the boil and boil rapidly for 10 min. Remove from the heat to test for the set. Boil until setting point is reached. Skim, pour into dry, warm jars and cover.

Most gooseberry jam turns a reddish colour as it cooks. It can be kept green by taking the following steps:

1 Choose a variety of gooseberry which is green when ripe, e.g. 'Careless', 'Green Gem' or 'Keepsake'.
2 Use a copper or brass preserving pan.
3 Give the jam the shortest possible boil in which it will set once the sugar has been dissolved.

For 'Muscat Flavoured' Gooseberry Jam, put the flowers from 8 heads of elderflowers in a muslin bag, and cook them with the gooseberries. Squeeze out the juice and remove the bag before the sugar is added. This is a good jam for beginners, because it is a notoriously good setter. It is specially good served on scones with whipped cream.

GOOSEBERRY AND STRAWBERRY JAM

1½ lb gooseberries,
weighed after they
have been topped
and tailed
1½ lb strawberries,
weighed after they
have been hulled
¼ pt water
3 lb sugar

Simmer the gooseberries in the water until they are tender. Add the strawberries and simmer a further 3–4 min. Add the sugar, stir over a low heat till dissolved, then boil rapidly until setting point is reached. Skim, pour into warm, dry jars and cover.

Yield—5 lb

GREENGAGE JAM

3 lb greengages   **3 lb sugar**
¼–½ pt water

Remove stalks and put the washed greengages into the pan with the water. Stew slowly until the fruit is well broken down. Ripe fruit or very juicy varieties will need only a small quantity of water and will be cooked in a few minutes. Firmer varieties may take about 20 min to break down, and will need the larger quantity of water. Add the sugar, stir over a low heat till dissolved, then boil rapidly, removing the stones as they rise to the surface (a stone-basket clipped to the side of the pan is useful for holding the stones, and allows any liquid to drip back into the pan). Keep testing for setting point after about 10 min rapid boiling. Skim, pot and cover.

Yield—5 lb

LOGANBERRY JAM

3 lb loganberries	3 lb granulated sugar

Cook the loganberries very gently—without any added water—until the centre core of the fruit is tender. Add the sugar, stir over a gentle heat until it is thoroughly dissolved. Boil rapidly until setting point is reached. Skim, pour into dry, warm jars and cover.

Yield—5 lb

MARROW JAM—PULPED

3 lb marrow
  (peeled and cut
  up)
2 lemons
¼ lb crystallized
  ginger
3 lb sugar

Steam the marrow until it is tender. Drain thoroughly and mash to a pulp. Grate the rind from the lemons and squeeze out the juice. Add rind, juice and the cut-up ginger to the marrow. Bring to the boil, add the sugar and stir over a low heat till the sugar is dissolved. Continue boiling, with frequent stirring, for about 20 min or until thick. Pour into warm, dry jars and cover.

Yield—approx 5½ lb

MARROW AND GINGER PRESERVE

4 lb marrow
  (weighed after
  preparation)
3 lb sugar
2 oz root ginger
3 tablesp lemon
  juice

Peel the marrow and cut into cubes, removing the seeds. Place the cubes in a colander over a pan of boiling water, put the pan lid on top of the marrow and steam until just cooked and tender. Place in a basin, cover with the sugar and leave overnight. Next day, bruise the root ginger (bang it with a hammer or weight) and tie it in muslin. Put the bag of ginger into a preserving pan with the marrow and lemon juice. Cook slowly for about 1 hr until the marrow is clear and transparent. This jam does not give a firm set, so do not hopefully go on cooking it. Stop cooking when the correct yield (5 lb) is obtained. By this time the marrow should be transparent and the syrup thick. Remove the bag of ginger just before the end. Pour into dry, warm jars and cover.

Yield—5 lb

MELON AND LEMON JAM

4 lb melon
  (weighed when
  prepared)
4 lemons
3 lb sugar

Peel the melon and remove the centre pith, reserving the pips. Cut the flesh into cubes. Wash the lemons, wipe dry and peel with a vegetable peeler to remove only the yellow rind. Cut the fruit in halves and squeeze out the juice. Strain off the juice into a small bowl. Put the lemon peel (yellow part only) and the pips and pulp from the squeezer and the pips from the melon into a loose muslin bag and add this to the melon in the preserving pan. Heat gently until the juice runs and then cook gently until the melon is tender and transparent (30–45 min). Remove the muslin bag. Add the lemon juice and sugar

Use red gooseberry jam to make a gay Swiss roll.

and stir without further heating until the sugar is completely dissolved. Bring to the boil and boil as rapidly as possible until a set is obtained. Pour into hot, dry jars and cover.

Yield—approx 5 lb

MULBERRY AND APPLE JAM—SIEVED

2½ lb mulberries
½ pt water
1 lb apples
  (peeled and
  cored)
3 lb sugar

Stew the mulberries in some of the water till soft. Rub through a sieve. Stew the apples in

the rest of the water. When soft, stir in the sieved mulberries and the sugar. Stir over a low heat till the sugar is dissolved. Bring to the boil and boil till 5 lb of jam is obtained.

Yields—5 lb

PEACH (FRESH) JAM (with added pectin)

2 lb yellow flesh
  peaches
¼ pt water
6 tablesp lemon
  juice
3 lb sugar
½ bottle pectin

Stone and skin the peaches and cut into

slices. Place in a large preserving pan with the water and the lemon juice. Cover the pan and simmer gently for 15–20 min until the fruit is tender. Add the sugar and stir over a low heat until the sugar has dissolved. Bring to a rolling boil and boil rapidly for 1 min stirring occasionally. Remove from the heat and stir in the pectin. Cool 5 min. Pot and put on waxed discs immediately. Cover and label.

Yield—5 lb

PINEAPPLE CONSERVE

1 lb pineapple	
(weighed after	
preparation)	
4 lemons	
¼ pt water	
1 lb sugar	

Peel the pineapple and cut the flesh into small neat cubes. Strain the juice of the lemons into a bowl, put the rind, pith and pips into a muslin bag. Put the cubes of pineapple, 4 tablesp juice from lemons and the muslin bag with the water into a pan. Allow to simmer gently until the cubes are completely tender. Remove the muslin bag and the pineapple cubes. Add the sugar and allow to dissolve. Return the pineapple to the syrup and cook until clear and the syrup thick. Pour into hot jars and cover as for jam.

Yield—approx 2 lb

PLUM JAM

3 lb plums	**¼–¾ pt water (¼ pt**
3 lb sugar	**for ripe, juicy**
	dessert plums,
	¾ pt for cooking
	varieties)

Remove stalks and put the washed plums into the pan with the water. Stew slowly until the fruit is well broken down. Ripe fruit or very juicy varieties will need only a small quantity of water and will be cooked in a few min. Firmer varieties may take about 20 min to break down, and will need the larger quantity of water. Add the sugar, stir over a

low heat till dissolved, then boil rapidly, remove the stones as they rise to the surface (a stone-basket clipped to the side of the pan is useful for holding the stones, and allows any liquid to drip back into the pan). Keep testing for setting point after about 10 min rapid boiling. Skim, pot and cover.

If desired, a few of the raw plums may be stoned; crack the stones, remove the kernels, blanch them by dipping in boiling water and add the halved kernels to the pan. For plum and apple jam, use 1½ lb plums and 1½ lb apples. Proceed as above.

Yield—5 lb

PLUM AND APPLE JAM

1½ lb plums	**¾ pt water**
1½ lb apples (pre-	**3 lb sugar**
pared weight)	

Wash the plums. Peel and core the apples. Stew the fruit slowly in the water until the skins of the plums are softened. Add the sugar, stir over a low heat till dissolved, bring to the boil and boil rapidly till setting point is reached.

Pour into warm dry jars and cover.

Note: As many stones as possible should be removed during cooking. Alternatively, the plums may be stoned before cooking.

Yield—5 lb

RASPBERRY JAM.
Quick Method

2½ lb raspberries	**3 lb granulated**
	sugar

This jam does not set very firmly, but it has a delicious fresh flavour. Do not wash the raspberries unless absolutely necessary; if they have to be washed, drain very thoroughly. Bring the fruit gently to the boil, then boil rapidly for 5 min. Remove from the heat, add the warmed sugar and stir well over a low heat until all the sugar has dissolved. Bring to the boil and boil rapidly for 1 min. Skim quickly, pour the jam at once into dry, warm jars and cover.

Yield—5 lb

RASPBERRY (or LOGANBERRY) AND RHUBARB JAM

2 lb rhubarb	$\frac{1}{4}$ pt water
1 lb raspberries OR loganberries	3 lb sugar

Wash and cut up the rhubarb and stew it gently in the water until it is reduced to a thick pulp. Meanwhile pick over the loganberries, add them to the rhubarb and simmer 5–10 min till tender. Add the sugar. If raspberries are being used, there is no need to cook them first—just add them with the sugar. Stir over a low heat till the sugar is dissolved. Bring to the boil and boil rapidly till setting point is reached. Skim. Pour into hot, dry jars and cover.

Yield—5 lb

RHUBARB AND FIG JAM

2 lb rhubarb	2 lb sugar
8 oz dried figs	Juice of 1 lemon

Cut the rhubarb into pieces and chop the figs into chunks. Mix with the sugar and lemon juice and leave to stand for 24 hr. Bring to the boil, and then boil rapidly to setting point. Cool for 15 min, stir well and pour into jars.

Yield—4 lb

RHUBARB AND GINGER JAM

3 lb rhubarb	1 oz bruised root ginger
3 lb sugar	
Juice of 3 lemons	

Wipe the rhubarb and cut it into chunks. Place it in a basin, sprinkling on the sugar in layers. Add the lemon juice and leave to stand overnight. Next day put the contents of the basin into a preserving pan and add the ginger, tied in muslin. Bring to the boil and boil briskly till the correct yield is obtained (see volume test).

Yield—5 lb

STRAWBERRY JAM

3$\frac{1}{2}$ lb hulled strawberries	Juice of 1 large lemon
3 lb sugar	

Heat the strawberries and lemon juice gently in the pan, stirring constantly to reduce the volume. Add the sugar, stir till dissolved and boil until setting point is reached. Remove the scum. Leave the jam undisturbed to cool until a skin forms on the surface and the fruit sinks (about 20 min). Stir gently to distribute the strawberries. Pour into warm, dry jars and cover immediately with waxed discs. Tie down when cold.

Yield—5 lb

WHOLE STRAWBERRY JAM (with added pectin)

2$\frac{1}{4}$ lb small strawberries	A little butter OR margarine
3 lb sugar	$\frac{1}{2}$ bottle pectin
3 tablesp lemon juice	

Hull the strawberries and put in a preserving pan with the sugar and lemon juice. Stand for 1 hr, giving the contents of the pan an occasional stir. Place over a low heat and, when the sugar has dissolved, add a small piece of butter or margarine to reduce foaming. Bring to a rolling boil and boil rapidly for 4 min. Remove from the heat and add the pectin. Stir well. Allow to cool for at least 20 min to prevent the fruit rising. Stir gently, then pour into clean, warm, dry jars. Put on waxed discs immediately. Cover and label when cold.

Yield—5 lb

PRESSURE-COOKER JAMS
APPLE GINGER JAM

3 lb green apples	$\frac{1}{2}$ pt water
1 large lemon	3 lb sugar
3 level teasp ground ginger	4 dessertsp crystallized ginger

Peel, core and cut the apples into quarters; tie the cores and peel in a muslin bag. Remove the trivet from the pressure cooker; put in the apples, rind and juice of the lemon, muslin bag, ground ginger and water. Cover the cooker, bring to 10 lb pressure over a *low* heat; cook for 5 min. Reduce pressure at room temperature. Remove the muslin bag. Return the cooker to the heat; add the sugar and stir until the sugar has dissolved. Add the finely chopped crystallized ginger; bring to boil and boil rapidly in the open cooker until setting point is reached. Pot and tie down immediately.

Yield—approx 4 lb

APRICOT (DRIED) or DRIED PEACH JAM

1 lb dried apricots	**3 lb sugar**
OR **dried peaches**	**Juice of 1 large**
1½ pt water	**lemon**

Wash the apricots or peaches; put the water to boil; put the sugar to warm. Remove the trivet from the pressure cooker. Put in the fruit, pour over the 1½ pt *boiling* water and allow to soak for 10 min. Bring to 15 lb pressure in the usual way and pressure cook for 10 min. Reduce pressure immediately with cold water, add lemon juice and warmed sugar and stir away from the heat, until the sugar is dissolved. Return the cooker to the heat and boil rapidly in the open cooker until setting point is reached. Skim, pot and tie down immediately. A few blanched, halved almonds may be added with the sugar.

Yield—approx 5 lb

BLACKBERRY AND APPLE JAM

2 lb blackberries	**Juice of 1 lemon**
1½ lb green apples	**3 lb sugar**
½ pt water	

Prepare and wash the blackberries. Peel and core the apples and tie peel and cores loosely in a muslin bag. Remove the trivet from the pressure cooker, then put in the blackberries, roughly sliced apples, the muslin bag and the water. Bring to 10 lb pressure in the usual way and pressure cook for 7 min. Reduce pressure at room temperature. Lift out the muslin bag, add the lemon juice and warmed sugar. Stir over a low heat until sugar is dissolved, then boil rapidly in the open cooker until setting point is reached. Pour into warm jars and cover in the usual way.

Yield—approx 5 lb

BLACKCURRANT JAM

2 lb blackcurrants	**2 lb sugar**
½ pt water	

Remove the stalks and wash the fruit. Remove the trivet from the pressure cooker. Pour the water into the cooker and add the blackcurrants. Cover, bring to 10 lb pressure and pressure cook for 3 min. Reduce pressure at room temperature. Remove cover and add sugar, stir until sugar has dissolved. Bring to the boil without the cover, and boil rapidly until a little will jell when tested on a cold plate. Pour into warmed jars and cover in the usual way.
Note: This needs only 3 min pressure cooking instead of the usual long simmer necessary to soften the skins in an ordinary pan.

Yield—approx 3 lb

DAMSON, PLUM or GREENGAGE JAM

3 lb fruit	**3½ lb sugar**
¼ pt water	

Wash, halve and stone the fruit. Remove kernels from some of the stones and blanch them. Remove the trivet from the pressure cooker, then add the fruit, water and kernels. Bring to 10 lb pressure in the usual way and pressure cook for 5 min. Reduce pressure at room temperature, add the warmed sugar. Return the cooker to the heat and stir until sugar is dissolved. Boil rapidly in the open cooker until setting point is reached (approx 10 min). Skim, pot and tie down immediately.

Yield—approx 5½ lb

MARROW GINGER JAM

4 lb marrow	4 lemons
½ pt water	2 oz root ginger
4 lb sugar	

Peel the marrow and cut flesh into cubes. Put the water in the pressure cooker, then the trivet and the prepared marrow. Bring to 15 lb pressure in the usual way and pressure cook 1–2 min according to the ripeness of the marrow. Reduce pressure immediately with cold water and transfer the marrow to a large bowl, adding the sugar, grated rind and juice of the lemons and the ginger, banged with a hammer to 'bruise' it, and tied in a muslin bag. Allow to soak for 24 hr. Next day, remove the trivet from the cooker, take out the ginger, return all other ingredients to the open cooker and bring slowly to boiling point, stirring well. Continue to boil until marrow is transparent and the syrup thick. Pot and tie down immediately.

Yield—approx 4 lb

MELON AND PINEAPPLE JAM

2 lb melon (weighed	Juice of 3 lemons
after preparation)	3 lb sugar
½ lb pineapple	
(weighed after	
preparation)	

Peel, core, cut the melon into small cubes and weigh out 2 lb. Peel, core and cut the pineapple into small cubes and weigh out ½ lb. Remove the trivet from the pressure cooker, then add the melon, pineapple and lemon juice. Bring to 10 lb pressure in the usual way and pressure cook 10 min. Reduce pressure at room temperature, then add the warmed sugar. Return the cooker to the heat and stir until the sugar is dissolved. Boil rapidly in the open cooker until setting-point is reached. Pot and tie down immediately.

Yield—4–4½ lb

Strawberry cake

PEACH (FRESH) JAM

3 lb fresh peaches	3 lb sugar
½ pt water	

Wash, halve and stone the fruit. Remove the kernels from some of the stones, blanch and halve. Remove trivet from the cooker, then add the fruit, kernels and water. Bring to 10 lb pressure in the usual way and pressure cook for 4 min. Reduce pressure at room temperature and add the warmed sugar. Return the cooker to the heat and stir until the sugar is dissolved. Boil rapidly in the open cooker until setting point is reached, 10–15 min approx. Allow the jam to stand until a skin forms, stir well, pot and tie down immediately.

Yield—approx 5 lb

Note: This is a useful—and delicious—jam to make during the times when there is little or no fresh fruit available.

PINEAPPLE AND APRICOT PRESERVE

1 pt water	Pinch of salt
1 lb dried apricots	2 lb sugar
1 lb canned pine-apple (crushed)	Juice of 1 lemon

Boil the water and pour over the washed apricots. Leave to soak for 15 min. Weigh out 1 lb of crushed pineapple. Remove the trivet from the pressure cooker and put in the soaked apricots and water, the pineapple and the salt. Bring to 10 lb pressure in the usual way and pressure cook for 10 min. Reduce pressure at room temperature. Return the cooker to the heat, without the lid, add the sugar and lemon juice and stir over a low heat until the sugar is dissolved. Boil rapidly until setting point is reached. Pot and tie down immediately.

Yield—approx 3½ lb

TOMATO JAM

1¾ lb tomatoes	1 lemon
¼ lb apples (sharp)	1 lb sugar

Scald the tomatoes, skin and cut them up. Peel, core and cut up apples. Put peel and core into a muslin bag. Remove the trivet from the pressure cooker. Put the tomatoes and apples into the cooker with the muslin bag and rind of the lemon and bring *slowly* to the boil without lid of cooker, stirring to prevent burning or sticking to bottom of cooker. Cover, bring to pressure, pressure cook for 5 min. Reduce pressure at room temperature. Lift out muslin bag and lemon rind. Return to heat, add warmed sugar and lemon juice, stir over low heat till sugar is dissolved and boil without the lid on the cooker, until a little will jell when tested on a cold plate.

Yield—approx 2 lb

Home-Made Jellies

JELLY-MAKING

1 Use fresh fruit, not over-ripe.

2 Simmer gently in the amount of water with the recipe till the fruit is tender and thoroughly broken down (usually $\frac{3}{4}$–1 hr). If in any doubt about its setting properties, test for pectin at this stage, as a good set depends upon the amount of acid, pectin and sugar present.

3 After cooking, strain the fruit through a jelly bag, first scalding the bag by pouring boiling water through it. Hang the bag on a special frame, or suspend it from the legs of an upturned stool *or* chair with a basin below to catch the drips.

4 Never hurry the straining of the juice by squeezing the bag; this may make the jelly cloud. Some people leave the juice to drip overnight, but do not leave it too long before completing the jelly, certainly not more than 24 hr. Fruit which is very rich in pectin can be strained twice. The two juices can be mixed together, or two grades of jelly can be made, one from the first and another from the second.

5 Measure the juice into a preserving pan. Bring to the boil. Add the sugar. Strained juice rich in pectin needs 1 lb sugar to each pint of juice. Juice with only a fair pectin content needs only $\frac{3}{4}$ lb sugar to each pint. A thick, sticky juice is almost certain to contain plenty of pectin, but many people prefer to be sure by using the Pectin Test above.

6 After dissolving the sugar, boil rapidly till setting point is reached (about 10 min). Test by any of the methods for Jam. The Flake Test, used with the Temperature Test, is probably the most satisfactory.

7 Skim, removing the last traces of scum from the surface with the torn edge of a piece of kitchen paper. Pour into warm jars, 1 lb size or smaller, at once, before it has time to begin setting in the pan. Put on waxed circles (waxed side down) immediately. Cover when hot or cold. Do not tilt the jars until the jelly has set. Store in a cool, dry, dark place.

The exact yield of jelly from each recipe cannot be given because of varying losses in straining the juice, but usually about 10 lb of jelly can be made from each 6 lb sugar used.

APPLE JELLY

4 lb well-flavoured crab-apples OR cooking apples (windfalls can be used)	Flavouring: lemon peel OR root ginger Sugar

Wash the apples and cut up without peeling or coring; just remove any bad portions. Barely cover with about 2–3 pt water and simmer with the chosen flavouring till tender and well mashed. This will take about 1 hr. Strain through a scalded jelly bag. Bring the strained juice to the boil and test for pectin. Add the sugar (usually 1 lb sugar to every pt of juice). Stir to dissolve. Boil briskly till setting point is reached.

BLACKBERRY AND APPLE JELLY

4 lb blackberries	2 pt water
4 lb cooking apples	Sugar

Rinse the fruit. Cut up the apples without peeling or coring. Simmer the blackberries and apples separately with the water for about 1 hr, until the fruits are tender. Mash well and allow to drip through a jelly bag. Measure the juice. Bring to the boil, then stir in the sugar (usually 1 lb to each 1 pt of juice). Boil briskly till set.

BLACKCURRANT JELLY

4 lb ripe black-currants	Sugar 2½ pt water

Remove the leaves and only the larger stems and wash the blackcurrants. Place in the preserving pan, add 1½ pt water, and simmer gently till thoroughly tender. Mash well, then strain the pulp through a scalded jelly bag, leaving it to drip undisturbed for at least 15 min. Return the pulp left in the jelly bag to the pan, add another pt of water and simmer for ½ hr. Tip this pulp back into the bag and allow to drip for 1 hr. Mix the first and second extracts together. Measure the juice into the cleaned pan, bring to the boil. Then add 1 lb sugar to each pt of juice and stir till dissolved. Boil briskly, without stirring, until setting point is reached. Remove the scum, then immediately pour the jelly into warm jars.

Apple jelly and mint jelly.

CRAB APPLE AND ROWANBERRY JELLY

1 lb crab-apples   **Sugar**
2 lb rowanberries

The rowanberries should be very ripe. Do not peel and core the crab-apples, but cut them up and put them into a pan with the berries removed from their stalks. Add just enough water to cover and simmer until the fruit is soft. Strain through a jelly bag and measure the juice. Allow 1 lb sugar to each pt of juice. Heat the juice gently, stirring in the sugar until dissolved. Boil hard to setting point and pour into hot jars. This can be used as a spread, or it can be eaten with roast lamb or game.

CRANBERRY AND APPLE JELLY

3 lb apples   **Water**
2 lb cranberries   **Sugar**

Rinse the fruit. Slice the apples, without peeling or coring, and place in a pan with the cranberries and sufficient water to cover. Simmer gently till thoroughly mashed. Test for pectin. Allow to drip through a jelly bag. Measure the juice. Allow usually 1 lb sugar to each pt of juice, but this depends on the pectin test. Bring the juice to the boil. Add the sugar and stir till dissolved, then boil briskly till setting point is reached.

DAMSON AND APPLE JELLY

6 lb apples   **4 pt water**
3 lb damsons   **Sugar**

Slice the apples, without peeling or coring, and add to the damsons and water. Simmer gently until the fruit is thoroughly mashed. Strain through a scalded jelly bag, allowing it to drip undisturbed. Return the juice to the pan, bring to the boil. Allow usually 1 lb sugar for each pt of juice, stir till dissolved, then boil briskly till setting point is reached.

28

Simple device for straining jelly.

ELDERBERRY AND APPLE JELLY

Equal weights of elderberries and sliced apples (not peeled or cored)	**Sugar**

Cook the elderberries and apples separately, with enough water just to cover the fruit. Simmer till tender and broken up. Test for pectin and if the set is poor reduce further. Strain the fruit through a scalded jelly bag. Measure the juices, mix, return to the pan and heat. Add ¾ lb sugar for every pt of juice. Stir till dissolved. Boil rapidly till setting point is reached.

GOOSEBERRY JELLY

4 lb green goose-berries	**Sugar** **2–3 pt water**

Wash the gooseberries and place them in the pan without topping and tailing. Add the water, cook till thoroughly tender and broken. Test for pectin. Strain through a scalded jelly bag and add ¾–1 lb of sugar to each pt of cold juice. (The amount depends on the results of the pectin test.) Bring to the boil, stirring to dissolve the sugar, and boil rapidly till setting point is reached.

Note: The addition of sugar to the cold juice allows it a longer boiling time and gives a darker, pleasanter colour to the jelly.

MINT JELLY

3 lb green apples **1⅛ pt water** **A small bunch of fresh mint** **1⅛ pt vinegar**	**Sugar** **3 level tablesp chopped mint** **A few drops of green colouring**

Wash the apples, cut in quarters and place in a preserving pan with the water and the bunch of mint. Simmer until the apples are soft and pulpy, then add the vinegar and boil for 5 min. Strain overnight through a cloth, measure the juice and to each pt, allow 1 lb sugar. Put the juice and sugar into the pan and bring to the boil, stirring until the sugar is dissolved. Boil rapidly until setting point is nearly reached, add the chopped mint and colouring, then boil until setting point is reached. Pour into hot jars and cover immediately with waxed discs. When quite cold, tie down with parchment or transparent covers, label and store.

ORANGE SHRED (APPLE) JELLY

(Rather mild in flavour, but a clear jelly with a delightful colour.)

3 lb apples (crab apples OR windfall apples)	Peel and juice of 3 oranges Sugar

Wash the apples and cut into rough pieces, discarding any bad portions. Place in a preserving pan with water barely to cover. Simmer gently until the fruit is quite tender (approx 1 hr). Strain through a scalded jelly bag. Meanwhile, wash the oranges and remove the peel in quarters. Cook the peel in ¼ pt water in a small covered saucepan for about 1 hr, or until tender. Measure the apple juice, remaining water from the cooked peel, and the strained juice of the oranges, and put into the preserving-pan with 1 lb sugar to each pt of liquid. Put over a low heat to dissolve the sugar and then boil fast until setting point is reached. Skim quickly. Meanwhile, dry the cooked peel in a cloth, and cut into fine shreds. Add these to the jelly immediately after skimming. Allow to cool slightly until a skin is formed on the surface of the jelly and then pour into hot, dry jars.

PLUM JELLY

2 lb Victoria plums	Juice of 2 lemons
½ pt water	Sugar

Simmer the plums in the water until they are soft. Strain through a jelly bag and measure the juice. Allow 1 lb sugar to each pt of juice. Add the sugar and lemon juice and heat slowly, stirring to dissolve the sugar. Boil hard to setting point and pour into hot jars.

QUINCE JELLY

Quinces	Sugar
Water	

Wipe the fruit carefully. Do not peel but cut into quarters and put into the preserving pan with sufficient cold water to cover. Bring slowly to the boil and simmer gently until the quinces are tender. Strain through a scalded jelly bag. Do not squeeze or the jelly will not be clear. Add 1 lb of sugar to each pt of juice and boil till setting point is reached.

RASPBERRY JELLY

8 lb raspberries	Sugar

Put the raspberries in the pan without any added water and heat gently until they are quite soft. Crush the fruit well. Strain through a scalded jelly bag. Return the measured juice to the clean pan, bring it to the boil and add 1 lb sugar to each pt of juice. Stir until the sugar is dissolved, then boil rapidly till setting point is reached.

REDCURRANT JELLY

6 lb large, juicy red OR red and white currants mixed	Sugar

Remove the leaves and only the larger stems. Place the cleaned fruit in the preserving pan, without any water, and heat very gently until the currants are softened for about ¾ hr and well cooked. Mash, then strain the pulp through a scalded jelly bag, leaving it to drip undisturbed. Measure the juice into the cleaned pan. Add 1¼ lb of sugar to each pt of juice. Bring to the boil, stirring constantly, and boil, without stirring, for 1 min. Swiftly skim the jelly and immediately pour it into the warmed jars, before it has a chance to set in the pan.

RHUBARB JELLY

3 lb rhubarb	3 lemons
1½ lb cooking apples	Sugar
3 pt water	Ground ginger OR cinnamon

Cut the rhubarb into pieces and put into a pan. Do not peel or core the apples, but cut them up and add to the rhubarb. Add the water and the grated rind and juice of the lemons. Simmer for 1 hr and strain through a jelly bag. Measure the juice and allow 1 lb sugar to each pt of juice. Heat the juice gently and stir in the sugar until dissolved. Add the chosen spice to your taste, and boil hard to setting point. Pour into hot jars.

SLOE AND APPLE JELLY

1 lb sloes	Peel of 2 lemons
6 lb cooking apples	Sugar

Put the sloes into a pan. Do not peel or core the apples, but cut them up and add them to the sloes, together with the lemon rind and just enough water to cover. Simmer for 1 hr. Strain through a jelly bag and measure the juice. Allow 1 lb sugar to each pt of juice. Heat the sugar and juice together gently, stirring until the sugar has dissolved. Boil hard to setting point and pour into hot jars.

PRESSURE-COOKER JELLIES

BLACKBERRY JELLY

2 lb blackberries	Sugar
½ pt water	Juice of 1 lemon

Wash the fruit. Remove trivet from the cooker and pressure cook the blackberries and water at 10 lb pressure for 5 min. Allow pressure to reduce at room temperature. Mash the fruit and strain through a fine jelly bag, allowing to drip undisturbed overnight. Allow 1 lb warmed sugar to each pt of juice. Add the strained lemon juice with the sugar. Stir over a low heat in the open cooker till the sugar is dissolved. Boil briskly till setting point is reached.

MEDLAR JELLY

4 lb medlars	4 lemons
1½ pt water	Sugar

Cut the washed fruit up roughly, peel the lemons thinly and squeeze out the juice. Remove the trivet from the pressure cooker. Put in the medlars, lemon rinds and water. Bring to 10 lb pressure in the usual way and cook for 30 min. Allow the pressure to reduce at room temperature. Strain the contents through a cloth, allowing to drip overnight if possible. Do not squeeze the cloth as this will cloud the jelly. Next day, measure the juice, return to the pan and add ¾ lb sugar to each pt of juice and the strained lemon juice. Stir over a low heat until the sugar is dissolved, then boil rapidly in the open cooker until setting point is reached.

MINT JELLY

2 lb sour green apples	1 pt water
	1 dessertsp
Large bunch of mint	vinegar
1 lemon	Sugar

Wash, peel and core the apples and cut in quarters. Wash the mint well. Remove the trivet from the pressure cooker and put in the apples, the mint (stalks as well), the thinly grated rind and juice of lemon, the water and the vinegar, Bring to 10 lb pressure over a medium heat and pressure cook for 8 min. Reduce pressure at room temperature and strain through a scalded fine muslin bag, leaving overnight if possible. Measure the juice, add 1 lb of warmed sugar to each pt. Stir over a low heat until the sugar is dissolved, bring to the boil and boil rapidly in the open cooker until setting point is reached. Pot and tie down immediately.
Note: A little very finely chopped mint may be added just before setting point is reached.

REDCURRANT JELLY

3 lb redcurrants	Sugar
½ pt water	

Wash the redcurrants and string them. Remove trivet from the cooker and pressure cook the fruit and water for 4 min at 10 lb pressure. Allow pressure to reduce at room temperature. Mash the fruit and allow to drip overnight through a scalded jelly bag. To every pt of juice add 1¼ lb of warmed sugar. Stir over low heat till the sugar has dissolved. Bring to the boil, and boil rapidly in the open cooker till setting point is reached.

ROSE HIP JELLY

| 2 lb rose hips | Sugar |
| 1½ pt water | Tartaric acid |

Choose firm but well-ripened fruit. Wash and top and tail. Remove the trivet from the pressure cooker. Put in the fruit and water. Bring to 10 lb pressure over a medium heat and pressure cook for 30 min. Reduce pressure at room temperature and stir well with a wooden spoon through a wire sieve. Strain the pulp again through a scalded jelly bag. Add 1 lb sugar and ½ teasp of tartaric acid to each pt of juice. Return to heat in open cooker. Stir over low heat until sugar is dissolved. Bring to boil and boil until setting point is reached.

Marmalades of Various Kinds

MARMALADE-MAKING

Marmalade-making is similar to jam-making and nearly all the same rules apply. As in jam-making, the fruit is first simmered gently, usually in an open pan, until it is thoroughly softened. During this long, slow cooking in the presence of acid, the jellying substance—pectin—is brought into solution. After this, the sugar is added and stirred over a gentle heat till dissolved. Then the marmalade is boiled rapidly, with a full, rolling boil, until setting point is reached. The tests for setting point are the same as for jam-making.

These are the essential differences:

(*a*) The peel of citrus fruit takes longer to soften than the fruit used for jams.

(*b*) Because most of the pectin is present in the pips and the pith, rather than in the fruit pulp or fruit juice, these are important ingredients of marmalade recipes. The pips and pith should not be discarded (unless they are being replaced by commercial pectin) but should be tied loosely in muslin and cooked with the fruit until the pectin has been extracted. If the muslin bag is tied to the handle of the pan, it can easily be removed before adding the sugar.

Further Points to Note for Making Marmalade

i All citrus fruits should be only just ripe, and must be used as soon as possible; if possible, order the fruit in advance and ask the greengrocer to tell you as soon as it reaches him.

Warmed redcurrant jelly glazes the raspberries and adds flavour to a pear custard in this flan.

2 It is not usually easy for the layman to distinguish between the true Seville orange and other imported bitter oranges. Sevilles are considered to have a superior flavour, but ordinary bitter oranges can replace them in the recipes below.

3 If the recipe tells you to peel the citrus fruit, try soaking the fruit in boiling water first for 1–2 min. This helps the skin to peel off easily.

4 It is necessary to use a very sharp stainless knife to cut the peel into shreds. Remember that the peel will swell slightly during the cooking. If large quantities of marmalade are made, it may be worth while buying a special machine which cuts the peel swiftly and easily.

Many recipes recommend soaking the peel, etc, for 24–48 hr to soften it before cooking. If time is limited, this is not essential. But if the soaking is omitted, you may have to cook the peel a little longer to make sure that it is sufficiently softened.

The sugar must not be added until the pulp is considerably reduced and the peel will disintegrate when squeezed. This takes $1\frac{1}{2}$–2 hr. Given this, setting point is generally reached after about 15–20 min rapid boiling.

How to Pot and Cover Marmalades

Always remove the scum from marmalade as soon as the setting point is reached. Use a hot metal spoon. If the scum is not removed immediately, it subsides gently on the peel and is then extremely difficult to skim off.

To prevent the peel rising to the top of the pots, leave the skimmed marmalade to cool undisturbed in the pan until a thin skin begins to form on the surface. Then stir it to distribute the peel (but do this gently to avoid air bubbles, and do not stir clear jelly marmalades).

Pour into the pots, using a small jug or cup.

Waxed discs should be placed on the marmalade immediately, taking care to avoid air bubbles under the disc. Some recipes advise putting on the outer cover when the marmalade is quite cold. Alternatively, the outer covers can be put

34

on while the marmalade is still very hot. But do not put them on when it is only warm, as warm marmalade makes moisture condense on the underside of the cover and the heat from the marmalade is not sufficient to dry it. Moulds grow easily on damp preserves.

CLEAR SHRED ORANGE MARMALADE

3 lb Seville oranges	**6 pt water**
2 lemons	**Sugar**
1 sweet orange	

Wash the fruit, dry and cut in half. Squeeze out the juice and strain, keeping back pulp and pips. Scrape all the white pith from the skins, using a spoon, and put pips, pulp and white pith into a bowl with 2 pt water. Shred the peel finely with a sharp knife and put this into another bowl with 4 pt water and the juice. Leave to stand for 24 hr. Strain the pips, etc, through a muslin bag and tie loosely. Put the bag and strained liquor, the peel and juice into the preserving pan and bring to simmering point. Simmer for 1½ hr until the peel is tender. Remove from the heat and squeeze out the muslin bag gently. For a very clear jelly, allow to drip only. Measure 1 lb sugar to each pt juice and allow the sugar to dissolve completely over a low heat. Bring to the boil and boil rapidly for about 20 min until a set is obtained. Remove from the heat and cool until a skin forms on the surface. Pour into hot jars and cover immediately.

Yield—approx 10 lb

DARK COARSE-CUT MARMALADE

2 lb Seville oranges	**6 lb sugar**
1 lemon	**1 tablesp black**
7 pt water	**treacle**

Wash the fruit, cut in half and squeeze the juice. Tie the pips loosely in a muslin bag. Slice the skins into medium-thick shreds. Put the juice, muslin bag, sliced peel and water into a preserving pan and simmer until the peel is tender and the liquid reduced by at least ⅓. This will take about 1½ hr. Remove the bag of pips, after squeezing the juice out gently. Remove the pan from the heat then add the sugar and the treacle; return the pan to the heat and stir over a low heat till the sugar is dissolved. Then boil rapidly till setting point is reached.

Yield—10 lb

FIVE FRUIT MARMALADE

2 lb fruit: 1 orange,	**3 pt water**
1 grapefruit, 1	**3 lb sugar**
lemon, 1 large	
apple, 1 pear	

Wash and skin orange, grapefruit and lemon and shred the peel finely. Cut this fruit coarsely. Put the pips and coarse tissue in a basin with ½ pt water. Place the peel and cut citrus fruit in a bowl with 2½ pt water. Soak for 24 hr. Strain the pips and tissue, tie in a muslin bag and place in a preserving pan with the fruit, the peel and the liquid. Peel and dice the apple and pear and add to the rest of the fruit. Bring to the boil, simmer for 1¼ hr and until reduced by ⅓. Remove the muslin bag. Add the sugar, stir over low heat until dissolved. Bring to the boil and boil rapidly until set. This takes about 30 min. Cool slightly, then pot into clean warm jars. Seal and label in the usual way.

You can make Three or Four Fruit Marmalade by using fewer kinds of fruit, e.g. 2 grapefruit, 2 lemons and 1 large sweet orange, or 2 oranges, 1 grapefruit, 1 apple and 1 pear.

Yield—5 lb

GRAPEFRUIT MARMALADE

1½ lb grapefruit	3 pt water
2 lemons	3 lb sugar

Wash the fruit, cut in half and squeeze out the juice. Remove some of the pith if it is thick, cut it up coarsely and put it with the pips in a muslin bag. Slice the peel finely. Put all the fruit and juice into a bowl, cover with the water and leave overnight. Next day put it all into a preserving pan and cook gently for 2 hr or until the peel is soft. Remove the bag of pips, add the sugar, stir until it is dissolved, then boil rapidly until setting point is reached. Pot and cover in the usual way.

Yield—5 lb

GRAPEFRUIT AND PINEAPPLE MARMALADE (with added pectin)

2 large grapefruit	1 can crushed
2 lemons	pineapple
¾ pt water	4 lb sugar
⅛ teasp bicarbonate of soda	1 bottle pectin

Wash the fruit and remove the skins in quarters. Shave off and discard the thick white part. Slice the rind very finely with a sharp knife and place in a preserving pan with the water and the bicarbonate of soda. Bring to the boil and simmer, covered, for 10 min, stirring occasionally. Meantime, cut up the peeled fruit, discarding the pips and coarse tissue. Add the juice, pulp and the can of crushed pineapple and juice and simmer, covered, for 15 min. Add the sugar, stir over low heat until the sugar is dissolved. Bring to a full rolling boil and keep it boiling fast for 3 min, stirring. Remove from the heat, stir in the pectin. Bring to the boil and boil 1 min. Cool for 10–15 min. Pour into clean, warm jars and seal at once.

Yield—6 lb

LEMON MARMALADE

1½ lb lemons	3 lb sugar
3 pt water	

Wash the lemons and shred the peel finely (removing some of the pith if very thick). Cut up the fruit, putting aside the pips and coarse tissue. Put the fruit and shredded peel in a large bowl with 2½ pt water. Put the pips, pith and coarse tissue in a basin covered with ½ pt water. Leave all to soak for 24 hr. Next day transfer all to the preserving pan, tying the pips, etc. in a muslin bag, bring to the boil and simmer gently for about 1½ hr, until the peel is tender and the contents of the pan are reduced by at least ⅓. Remove the muslin bag. Add the sugar, stir until dissolved, then bring to the boil and boil rapidly till setting point is reached (approx 15–20 min).

Yield—approx 5 lb

LEMON AND GINGER MARMALADE

1½ lb lemons	3 lb sugar
3 pt water	8 oz crystallized
2 oz root ginger	ginger

Wash and peel the lemons in quarters, cut the peel in fine shreds and place in a large bowl. Cut the fruit finely, putting aside the pips and coarse tissue. Put the fruit with the cut peel and cover with 2½ pt water. Put the pips and coarse tissue into a basin with ½ pt water. Soak for 24 hr.

Drain the liquid from the pips and tissue and place in a preserving-pan with the rest of the fruit and liquid. Tie the tissue, pips and root ginger in a muslin bag and add to the pan. Bring to the boil, reduce the heat and simmer gently for 1¼–1½ hr and until reduced by ⅓. Remove muslin bag. Add the sugar and finely-chopped crystallized ginger and place over low heat, stirring until sugar has dissolved. Bring to the boil and boil rapidly until setting point is reached, approx 20 min. Cool 5–10 min. Pot into clean jars. Cover and label.

Yield—5 lb

LEMON JELLY MARMALADE

2 lb lemons	3 lb sugar
3¼ pt water	

Cutting up oranges.

Adding measured water

Measuring sugar.

Putting into pots.

Scrub the lemons and wipe dry. Peel off the outer yellow skin, using a vegetable peeler or sharp knife, and cut the peelings into fine shreds. Tie these in a muslin bag. (N.B. If a marmalade with fewer shreds is preferred, add the shredded peel from only half the lemons.) Cook the shreds in 1½ pt of water, in a covered pan, until tender. Meanwhile, roughly cut up the fruit and cook with the remaining water in a preserving pan for 2 hr, with the lid on the pan. Pour off the liquid from the shreds, add it to the cooked fruit and strain it all through a scalded jelly bag. Pour the strained liquid into the rinsed preserving pan, simmer a little if it seems rather thin, then add the sugar and stir over a low heat till dissolved. Add the shreds and boil hard until setting point is reached.

LEMON SHRED JELLY MARMALADE (with added pectin)

1 tablesp very finely shredded lemon peel	¾ cup lemon juice (4–5 lemons)
1 pt water	2 lb 10 oz sugar
⅛ level teasp bicarbonate of soda	1 bottle pectin

Cook the peel in the water and bicarbonate

37

of soda for 10 min. Add the lemon juice and sugar and heat gently until the sugar has dissolved, stirring occasionally. Bring to a full rolling boil and boil rapidly for ½ min. Remove from the heat and add the pectin. Reboil for ½ min. Allow to cool slightly to prevent the fruit floating and skim if necessary. Pot and cover.

Yield—approx 4½ lb

MELON AND LEMON MARMALADE

Juice and rind of	1 lb melon,
1¼ lb lemons	prepared and
¼ pt water	cut in cubes
⅛ teasp bicarbonate	3 lb sugar
of soda	1 bottle pectin

Wash the fruit. Squeeze the juice from the lemons, remove most of the pith and shred the rinds very finely. Measure ¼ pt water into pan, add juice, rinds and the bicarbonate of soda. Simmer, covered, for 10 min. Add cubed melon, simmer till tender and transparent. Add sugar, heat gently till dissolved, stirring occasionally. Bring to full rolling boil quickly and boil for 2 min. Remove from heat, stir in pectin. Leave to cool for a few minutes to prevent fruit rising. Skim if necessary. Stir, pot and cover.

Yield—approx 4½ lb

ORANGE JELLY MARMALADE

2 lb Seville oranges	Juice of 2 lemons
4½ pt water	3 lb sugar

Peel the oranges, remove the thick pith and shred finely 4 oz of the rind. Cook the shreds in 1 pt water, in a covered pan, until tender (approx 1½ hr). Meanwhile, roughly cut up the fruit and put it with the lemon juice and 2½ pt water in a pan. Simmer for 2 hr, with the lid on the pan. Drain the liquid from the shreds, add it to the cooked fruit and strain it all through a scalded jelly bag. After it has dripped for ¼ hr, return the pulp to the preserving pan and add 1 pt water. Simmer for 20 min, then strain again through the jelly bag, allowing it to drip undisturbed.

Pour the strained liquid into the rinsed preserving pan, simmer a little if it seems rather thin, then add the sugar and stir over a low heat till dissolved. Add the shreds and boil hard until setting point is reached.

Yield—5 lb

SEVILLE ORANGE MARMALADE (1)

1½ lb Seville oranges	Juice of 1 lemon
4 pt water	Sugar

Wash the fruit and cut it in half. Squeeze out the juice and the pips. Cut the peel into shreds. Tie the pips in a muslin bag and put into a bowl with the orange and lemon juice, water and peel. Soak for 24–48 hr, covered to keep it clean. Transfer to the pan and cook for approx 1½ hr until the peel is soft. Remove the bag of pips, squeezing it gently. Take the pan from the heat, add 1 lb sugar to each pt and stir till dissolved. Return pan to heat, bring to the boil; boil rapidly until setting point is reached.

Yield—approx 6½ lb

SEVILLE ORANGE MARMALADE (2)

1½ lb Seville oranges	Juice of 1 lemon
2 pt water	3 lb sugar

Wash the fruit and put it whole and unpeeled into a saucepan. Pour on 2 pt boiling water and simmer gently with the lid on the pan until the fruit is tender enough to be pierced easily with a fork (approx 2 hr). (Alternatively, the whole fruit and water can be baked in a covered casserole in a cool oven until the fruit is soft; this will take about 4–5 hr.) When the fruit is tender, cut it in half and remove pips then cut up the fruit with a knife and fork, carefully retaining all the juice. Return the pips to the water in which the fruit was cooked, and boil for 5 min to extract more pectin. Put the sliced fruit with the liquid (strained free from pips) and lemon juice in the preserving pan. Reduce the heat, add the sugar and stir till dissolved. Bring to the boil and boil rapidly till setting point is reached.

Note: This method is simple to do and is recommended if a fairly coarse-cut marmalade is liked.

Yield—5 lb

SEVILLE ORANGE MARMALADE (3)

1½ lb Seville oranges	Juice of 1 lemon
3 pt water	3 lb sugar

Wash the oranges and, with a sharp knife, shred finely. Tie the pips and pieces of coarse tissue in a muslin bag. Put fruit, muslin bag and water in a basin and leave overnight. Next day transfer to the preserving pan, bring to the boil, add the lemon juice, and simmer gently till the peel is soft and the contents of the pan are reduced by at least ⅓ (approx 1½–2 hr). Remove the muslin bag, after squeezing gently. Add the sugar, stir over low heat till dissolved, then bring to the boil and boil rapidly till setting point is reached. Skim. Allow to cool for about 10 min before potting.

Yield—5 lb

SEVILLE ORANGE AND GINGER MARMALADE

1¼ lb Seville oranges	3½ pt water
1 lemon	8 oz crystallized
1 oz root ginger	ginger
	Sugar

Wash the oranges and lemon, cut in halves and squeeze out the juice and pips. Strain the juice into a bowl and tie the pips with the root ginger in a muslin bag. Cut the peel into shreds, thickness according to preference, and put with the juice, water and bag of pips in the bowl. Leave to soak overnight. Next day, put into a preserving pan, bring to the boil and simmer gently until the peel is quite soft (about 1½–2 hr). Remove the bag of pips after squeezing gently. Cut the crystallized ginger into ¼-in cubes and add to the cooked peel. Remove from the heat and measure. Add 1 lb of sugar to each pt of fruit. Stir over a gentle heat until the sugar

is dissolved and then boil rapidly until setting point is reached.

Yield—approx 6½ lb

TANGERINE MARMALADE (with added pectin)

3 lb tangerines	5 lb sugar
2 pt water	1 bottle pectin
Juice of 3 lemons	

Wash the tangerines and put into a preserving pan with the water. Simmer gently, covered, for 40 min. When cool enough to handle, remove peel and cut up fruit, taking out the pips and the very coarse tissue. Return the pips and tissue to the liquid and boil hard for 5 min. Shred half the peel, discard the rest. Strain the liquid, discarding the pips and tissue, and put back in the preserving pan with the pulp, peel, lemon juice and sugar. Stir over gentle heat until the sugar has dissolved and then bring to a full rolling boil. Boil hard for 3 min. Remove from heat, stir in pectin, boil for 1 min. Skim if necessary. Cool slightly and pot in the usual way.

Note: Tangerine Marmalade is normally a difficult one to set; the addition of pectin gives an easy method.

Yield—approx 7 lb

THREE FRUIT MARMALADE

About 1½ lb fruit—	3 pt water
1 grapefruit, 2 lemons and 1 sweet orange	3 lb sugar

Wash and peel the fruit, and shred the peel coarsely or finely according to taste. (Remove some of the pith if it is very thick.) Cut up the fruit, tying the pips and any pith or coarse tissue in a muslin bag. Soak the fruit, peel and muslin bag in the water in a bowl for 24 hr. Next day, transfer to the preserving pan and simmer gently for 1½ hr or until the peel is tender and the contents of the pan are reduced by about ⅓. Remove the muslin bag, after squeezing gently. Add the sugar, stir over a low heat till dissolved. Bring to the boil and boil rapidly till setting point is reached.

Yield—5 lb

PRESSURE-COOKER MARMALADES

In order to soften the peel sufficiently, marmalade making has to be a lengthy process; the cooking time (which may normally be about $1\frac{1}{2}$–2 hr) can be shortened to about 7–10 min if a pressure cooker is used. The preliminary cooking to soften the peel is done in the closed pan. The sugar is then added and the cooking finished in the open pan.

Note: Some types of pressure cooker will not make more than 5 lb of marmalade at a time. The pressure cooker must not be more than $\frac{1}{2}$ filled when ready for pressure cooking.

GRAPEFRUIT MARMALADE

2 lb fruit (approx)—	$1\frac{1}{2}$ pt water
4 lemons and 2 grapefruit	3 lb sugar

Scrub the lemons, shred finely and put the pips on one side. Scrub the grapefruit and peel; remove the thick white pith and the pips, and tie with the lemon pips in a muslin bag. Shred the grapefruit peel finely. Shred the grapefruit coarsely. Remove the trivet from the pressure cooker. Put into the cooker the water, all the prepared fruit, the peel and the muslin bag. Bring to 10 lb pressure in the usual way and pressure cook for 10 min. Reduce pressure at room temperature, remove the muslin bag and add the sugar. Return the open cooker to the heat, stir over low heat until the sugar is completely dissolved. Bring to the boil and boil rapidly until setting point is reached.

Yield—approx 5 lb

LEMON MARMALADE

1 lb lemons	$2\frac{1}{2}$ lb sugar
1 pt water	

Wash the fruit and shred, but not too finely. Remove pips and tie in a muslin bag. Remove the trivet from the pressure cooker and put in the fruit, water and the muslin bag. Bring to 10 lb pressure in the usual way, and pressure cook for 7 min. Reduce pressure at room temperature, remove the bag of pips and add the sugar. Return cooker to the heat and stir until sugar is dissolved. Boil rapidly in the open cooker until setting point is reached.

Yield—4–$4\frac{1}{2}$ lb

LEMON JELLY MARMALADE

2 lb lemons	3 lb sugar
$2\frac{1}{2}$ pt water	

Make as for Orange Jelly Marmalade, substituting lemons for oranges.

Note: No soaking of the fruit is necessary, and it is softened in 20 min (compared with about 2 hr by ordinary cooking). In spite of the quick cooking, the jelly is full of flavour.

LIME MARMALADE

Important: The limes should not be used whilst they are still bright green and obviously unripe. They will only give a bitter marmalade, very difficult to set. Put them on one side and leave till they turn yellowish and very slightly shrivelled.

1 lb limes	$1\frac{1}{3}$ lb sugar
$1\frac{1}{4}$ pt water	

Take the peel off half the fruit. Remove the pith from the peel, shred the peel finely and tie loosely in a small piece of muslin. Cut the limes up roughly. Remove trivet from the cooker, put in fruit, pith, water and muslin bag. Bring to 10 lb pressure and cook for 20 min. Allow pressure to reduce at room temperature. Strain through a fine sieve or jelly bag. Return the strained liquid to the cooker, add the sugar, stir over a low heat till dissolved. Boil rapidly for 3–5 min. Skim. Wash shreds from muslin bag in a sieve with plenty of water to separate them. Add to the marmalade. Continue boiling until setting point is reached.

Five fruit marmalade.

Yield—2–2⅓ lb
This recipe can be doubled exactly, but if trebled the amount of water required is only 3½ pt not 3¾ pt.

ORANGE JELLY MARMALADE

Note: No soaking of the fruit is necessary, and it is softened in 20 min (compared with about 2 hr by ordinary cooking). In spite of the quick cooking, the jelly is full of flavour.

2 lb Seville OR	**2½ pt water**
sweet oranges	**3 lb sugar**
Juice and pips from	
3 lemons	

Wash the fruit; peel 2 of the oranges very thinly, carefully removing all the pith; shred the peel very finely and tie it loosely in a muslin bag. Roughly chop the 2 peeled oranges, together with the unpeeled oranges and put into the pressure cooker (from which the trivet has been removed). Add the lemon pips, the orange pips and pith, the muslin bag and the water. Bring to 10 lb pressure in the usual way, and pressure cook for 20 min. Allow the pressure to reduce at room temperature. Remove the muslin bag and wash the shreds thoroughly in a strainer under cold water. Strain all the rest through a scalded jelly bag or double thickness of linen tea towel, waiting until all the liquid has dripped through (do not hurry the straining by squeezing as this will cloud the jelly). Rinse out the pressure cooker. Return to it the strained liquid, and heat slightly. Add the warmed sugar and strained lemon juice, stir over a low heat until dissolved. Bring to boil and boil rapidly in the open cooker for 5–10 min. Skim thoroughly. Add shreds and boil till setting point is reached.

Yield—approx 4 lb

SEVILLE ORANGE MARMALADE

2 lb Seville oranges	**4 lb sugar**
2 pt water	**Juice of 2 lemons**

Wash the oranges and remove the peel and pips. Cut the fruit up roughly. Shred the peel according to taste. Tie the pips in a muslin bag. Remove the trivet from the pressure cooker, then add the prepared oranges, peel, muslin bag and water. Bring to 10 lb pressure in the usual way and pressure cook for 10 min. Reduce pressure at room temperature, remove the bag of pips, and add warmed sugar and strained lemon juice. Return cooker to heat and stir until sugar is dissolved. Boil in the open cooker until setting point is reached (approx 7 min).

Yield—approx 6¼ lb

TANGERINE JELLY MARMALADE

3 lb tangerines OR	**3 lemons**
mandarins	**3 pt water**
1 grapefruit	**4 lb sugar**

Wash all the fruit. Peel 8 of the tangerines

or mandarins and be sure that all the pith is removed. Shred this peel finely, and tie loosely in a muslin bag. Chop up the 8 tangerines and the rest of the unpeeled, unpipped fruit and put together with the muslin bag and the water into a pressure cooker, from which the trivet has been removed. Bring to 10 lb pressure in the usual way and cook for 12 min. Allow the pressure to reduce at room temperature then continue as for Orange Jelly Marmalade.

Yield—approx 5½ lb

THREE FRUIT MARMALADE

Approx 2 lb fruit—	**1½ pt water**
2 oranges, 1 grape-	**4 lb sugar**
fruit and 2 lemons	

Cut the washed fruit in quarters. Remove pips and tie loosely in a muslin bag. (**Note:** do not use 'seedless' fruit, otherwise a good set will not be obtained.) Remove the trivet from the pressure cooker; add the prepared fruit and the water and muslin bag. Bring to 10 lb pressure in the usual way and pressure cook for 7 min. Reduce pressure at room temperature. Remove the muslin bag and chop the fruit, either coarsely or finely according to taste. Return the fruit to the cooker, replace on the heat and add the sugar, stirring over low heat until it is dissolved. Boil rapidly in the open cooker until setting point is reached.

Yield—approx 6½ lb

Fruit 'Butters', 'Cheeses' and Curds

FRUIT BUTTERS AND CHEESES

There are two thick preserves of fruit pulp and sugar, known as 'butters' and 'cheeses'. These two products are often confused. 'Butters' are thick and semi-set, like stiffly whipped cream, which can be spread. 'Cheeses' should be much firmer, as they were originally made to be turned out and sliced (often for 'packed meals' for farm workers in the fields). Both types should look thick and glossy.

Both are useful mixtures for using up a glut crop or large quantity of fruit, or windfalls, as the sheer bulk is reduced considerably in cooking.

'Butters' normally contain half the amount of sugar to fruit pulp; 'cheeses' need equal quantities of sugar and pulp. It is best to put both preserves into small jars with wide mouths. A 'butter' is ready for potting when a little can be put on to a plate and no rim of liquid appears round the edge of the mixture. A 'cheese' is tested by drawing a spoon across the bottom of the pan until it leaves a clear line. After potting it can be left for some time, even a year, before being eaten. It will then be firm enough to slice in the old way; and it is excellent for eating with bread, cheese and pickles, in a packed meal or on a picnic, instead of butter.

These 'cheeses' can also be turned out to cut in slices to eat with cream or with milk puddings. Most of them are also good to eat with meat, poultry or game instead of chutney.

APPLE OR PEAR SPICE BUTTER

6 lb apples OR pears	2 level teasp
2 pt cider OR perry	allspice
Granulated sugar	½ teasp nutmeg
Lemon juice and	2 level teasp
grated rind	cloves

Wash and cut up the fruit. Put in a pan with the cider or perry, and cook over a low heat until tender. Pass through a sieve. Weigh the pulp and allow 1 lb sugar and the rind and juice of 1 lemon for every 1 lb of pulp. Add the remaining ingredients and cook over a low heat for 40–60 min, until thickened. Turn into hot sterilized jars. Seal when cold.

APPLE AND CHESTNUT BUTTER

Windfalls OR cooking apples
Ground cinnamon OR cooked chestnut
pulp to taste (OR BOTH)

Core the apples. Chop them roughly. Simmer in the least possible amount of water, and when soft, process in an electric blender (or sieve) to make apple-sauce or purée. Place this purée in a large pot over very low heat and cook for 6–8 hr. (There are varying opinions about this; some people say 3–4 hr is enough, others say the 'butter' will only be stiff enough after about 20 hr.
If preferred, place in the oven overnight, or leave in the oven for several days, well covered; cook until the mixture is dark, thick and pasty. Bottle in sterile jars, and seal.

APPLE AND PLUM BUTTER

3 lb apples	Sugar
1 lb plums	

Peel and core the apples and cut them up. Cook them in very little water until soft. Stone the plums and add them to the apples. Cook until the plums are soft and then sieve the mixture. Weigh the pulp and allow 12 oz sugar to each 1 lb of pulp. Stir in the sugar

until dissolved and boil until thick and creamy. Pour into hot jars and cover.

BLACKBERRY CHEESE

4 lb ripe blackberries	Sugar
2 teasp citric OR	
tartaric acid	

Wash the blackberries. Put them into a pan with just enough water to cover them, and the acid. Bring them to the boil and simmer gently until the fruit is soft. Put through a sieve and weigh the pulp. Allow 1 lb sugar to each lb of pulp, and stir in the sugar until dissolved. Boil and stir until the mixture is thick. Pour into hot jars and cover.

CHERRY BUTTER

4 lb black cherries	2 lb sugar
1 lemon	

Remove the stones from the cherries. Take the kernels from a few of them, blanch and skin them. Put the cherries in a bowl in layers with the sugar, and the grated rind and juice of the lemon. Leave to stand overnight. Simmer for 20 min. Add the kernels and then boil very quickly until thick, stirring well. Pour into small hot jars and cover.

GOOSEBERRY CHEESE

3 lb green goose-	½ pt water
berries	Sugar

Top and tail the gooseberries. Simmer them in water until soft, and then sieve them. Weigh the pulp, and allow 12 oz sugar to each lb pulp. Stir the sugar into the fruit pulp until it has dissolved. Bring to the boil, and then cook gently until the mixture is thick, stirring all the time. Pour into hot jars and cover.

GRAPE BUTTER

3 lb black grapes	Sugar

44

Lemon Curd.

Wash the grapes and simmer them in just enough water to cover until they are soft. Put through a sieve and weigh the pulp. Allow 8 oz sugar to each lb grape pulp. Cook the pulp until thick. Add the sugar and stir until dissolved. Bring the mixture to the boil, then cook gently, stirring well until creamy. Pour into hot jars and cover.

MAGGIE'S SPICED APPLE BUTTER

Windfalls and withered apples	$\frac{1}{8}$–$\frac{1}{4}$ teasp ground cloves per pt
$\frac{1}{2}$ lb light brown sugar per pt of pulp	of pulp OR to taste
$\frac{1}{4}$–$\frac{1}{2}$ teasp ground cinnamon per pt of pulp OR to taste	

Cut the apples into four. Cut out bruised and bad portions, but do not core or peel them. Place them in a large earthenware or iron crock with about $\frac{1}{4}$ pt hot water or cider. Cover the crock with aluminium foil, then with a lid or plate. Place it in the oven at a low heat (110 °C, 225 °F, Gas $\frac{1}{4}$) and leave it for 5–6 hr or overnight.

Sieve the softened apples, and measure the pulp. (This easily-made pulp is an excellent purée for apple sauce as it stands.)

Add the sugar to the hot apples and stir it in thoroughly. Place over moderate heat, bring almost to the boil, and simmer for $\frac{3}{4}$–1 hr until the 'butter' is dark and stiff. Ten minutes before the end of the cooking time, add the spices and stir them in. At the same time, place jars to heat gently in the oven.

At the end of the cooking time, remove the apple pulp from the heat. Spoon it into the hot jars. Leave until cold. Cover with circles of waxed paper, then with screw-on or other airtight seal. Label and date.

Ideally this butter should be kept for at least a year (even two) before use. It is stiffer than jam, and after a year or so is even spicier and stiffer. After two years it can be cut in slices like a Swiss Roll—which is how peasant farming folk used to eat it in days gone by. Today it makes just as good a part of a packed or picnic lunch as it did then.

Making fruit 'butters' was an annual task for the peasant and farming wives of mediæval Europe, and 'apple butter' was made throughout the orchard lands of Germany and Holland, to preserve the fruit in compact form for winter use.

Naturally, then, when they were driven into

45

exile, the non-conformist 16th-century peasant and farming peoples of these lands included it among their supplies and carried the knowledge of how to make it with them. One group of these exiles, called the Schwenkfelders, some 200 years later, set off for America in 1734. After the usual grim voyage in appalling conditions, they reached their destination in September, and tasted fresh water, bread and apples for the first time in nearly three months. So every September since then, they have held a Thanksgiving Service, a 'Gedaechtnisz Tag', at which they take water, bread, butter and apple butter. The following recipe is based on theirs.

SPICED APPLE BUTTER, AMERICAN STYLE

3 pt medium sweet cider	¼ teasp ground cloves
2 lb ripe dessert apples	⅛ teasp ground allspice
4 oz light brown OR Demerara sugar	⅛ teasp salt
¼ teasp ground cinnamon	

Cook the cider fairly fast for ½–¾ hr until reduced by half. Add the quartered and cored (but not peeled) apples, reduce the heat and simmer until the apples are very soft. Scoop them into a sieve with a perforated spoon, and sieve them straight back into the hot cider. Add and stir in the sugar and spices. Simmer the pulp, stirring frequently, until the 'butter' is dark and stiff. Alternatively, place the pot in the oven at a heat of not more than 150 °C, 300 °F, Gas 2, for 5–6 hr or overnight. Leave the pot uncovered. During the last ¾–1 hr of cooking time, heat jars in the oven.

Yield—1½ pt

FRUIT CURDS

Curds are fruit-flavoured creamy mixtures made with egg, butter and sugar cooked with fruit juices or pulp. They should be made with castor sugar and unsalted butter cooked in a double saucepan, or in a bowl over hot water. Ideally the fruit juices and the beaten eggs should be strained before adding to the butter and sugar mixture. A curd should be cooked gently over low heat, and stirred well. It is ready when the mixture is creamy and coats the back of a spoon, and the mixture will thicken as it cools.

Curds should be used within 1–2 months as their storage-life is short. They should be made in small quantities and stored in small jars, kept in a cool dark place. They make excellent tart fillings and spreads, sauces for ices and puddings, and can be added to butter icings for filling sponge cakes.

APPLE CURD

1½ lb sharp cooking
 apples
¼ pt water
Juice of 1 lemon
2 eggs
4 oz butter
12 oz sugar
Pinch of ground
 ginger

Peel and slice the apples, and simmer them in water and lemon juice to a pulp. Put through a sieve. Beat the eggs well and add to the apples, butter and sugar. Heat in a double saucepan until the curd thickens but does not boil. Add the ginger, pot and cover at once. This will keep for 2–3 months.

APRICOT CURD

8 oz fresh apricots	8 oz castor sugar
1 lemon	2 eggs
2 oz butter	

Put the apricots in a pan with very little water and cook until soft. Sieve the fruit and add the pulp to the grated rind and juice of the lemon, butter, sugar and well-beaten eggs. Cook in a double saucepan, stirring well, until the curd thickens. Pour into hot jars and cover. This will keep for 2 months.

GOLDEN CURD

2 oz butter	8 oz sugar
2 oranges	4 eggs
1 lemon	

Melt the butter in a double saucepan. Grate the orange and lemon rinds finely. Squeeze out the juices and strain. Add the grated rinds and strained juice to the sugar and the butter and stir over gentle heat until the sugar dissolves. Cool slightly and stir in well-beaten eggs. Return to the heat and cook gently, stirring until the mixture thickens and coats the back of a spoon. Pour into hot jars and cover. This will keep 1 month.

GOOSEBERRY CURD

3 lb green gooseberries	1½ lb castor sugar
¾ pt water	4 oz butter
	4 eggs

Top and tail the gooseberries and cook them in water until soft. Put through a sieve, and put the fruit pulp into a double saucepan. Add the sugar, butter and well-beaten eggs and stir over gentle heat until the mixture thickens. Pour into hot jars and cover. This will keep 1 month.

LEMON OR ORANGE CURD

4 eggs	Rind and juice of
2 oz butter	2 oranges and
8 oz loaf sugar	1 lemon

Whisk the eggs and put into a basin with the butter, sugar, finely-grated lemon rind (or orange rind) and the strained juice. Place the basin over a pan of boiling water, stir until the mixture is thick and smooth. Pour into clean, warm jars and cover.

LEMON CURD (pressure cooker)

2 eggs	2 oz butter OR
½ lb granulated sugar	margarine
	2 lemons

Beat the eggs well in a heatproof glass or china bowl. Add the sugar and the fat cut into small pieces. Add the grated rind and strained juice of the lemons. Stir all well together. Put ½ pt water in the pressure cooker, plus 1 tablesp vinegar (the vinegar prevents discoloration of the inside of the cooker). Cover the basin with 2 layers of greaseproof paper, tied on with string. Stand the basin on the trivet in the cooker. Bring to 15 lb pressure in the usual way and pressure cook for 10 min. Allow the pressure to reduce gradually at room temperature. Stir the curd very thoroughly, pour into a warm, dry jar, cover with a waxed disc and tie down immediately.

Yield—1 lb

Fruits and Herbs Bottled and Dried

FRUIT BOTTLING

From many successful bottling methods, we have chosen two to give in detail. The *Quick Deep Pan* method is probably the most useful for a busy housewife who wishes to complete a large amount of bottling in the shortest possible time. The *Slow Deep Pan* method is recommended for anyone who wants to display for exhibitions, as this method is more likely to produce jars which look perfect.

Preparing and Testing Jars

There are two main types of preserving jar—one which fastens with a screwband and the other fastening with clips or grips. Some are straight sided, for easy packing, others have a 'shoulder'. Jam jars can be used, if fastened with special covers.

Always examine your jars before use to see that they are unchipped. If the lid or the rim of the jar is chipped, discard it since it will not have an airtight seal. Do not use metal covers if they are bent or if the lacquer has been attacked by fruit acid. It is not advisable to use rubber rings a second time. Test unused rubber rings by stretching them: if they are good, they feel elastic and should return to normal size.

Before filling the jars, wash them thoroughly and drain them. Do not wipe dry.

Early summer bottlings.

Preparing Syrup or Brine

Fruit can be preserved in plain water, but a sugar syrup gives a better flavour and colour. The quantity of sugar used for a sugar syrup can be varied to suit your taste, but the usual quantity for most fruits is 8 oz granulated or loaf sugar to each 1 pt of water. Heat together and, when dissolved, bring to boiling-point and boil for 1 min. (If the syrup is to be used cold, save cooling time by heating the sugar with half the water and then adding the rest of the water cold.) If it is to be kept hot for long, put the lid on the pan to prevent evaporation.

If you prefer, substitute equal weights of *golden syrup* or *honey* for sugar. You can also add spices such as cinnamon or nutmeg.

To prepare brine for bottling tomatoes—add $\frac{1}{2}$ oz salt to each 1 qt of water. Bring to the boil and boil for 1 min.

Choosing, Preparing and Packing the Fruit

Choose fresh, firm, ripe fruit (except gooseberries, which should be green and hard). It is a waste of time and labour to bottle damaged or over-ripe fruit. Grade according to size, so that fruit of the same size is packed into each jar. If necessary, use the handle of a wooden spoon to help to place firm fruit in position. To ensure a tight pack for

49

soft fruit, tap the filled jars on a folded cloth or on the palm of your hand.

Deal with the fruits below, as follows:

Apples Peel, core, cut into slices, or rings $\frac{1}{4}$ in thick. To prevent discoloration drop them into brine (1 oz salt to 4 pt water), keeping them under the surface with a plate. Drain, rinse and pack immediately.

Apples (Solid Pack) After draining from brine as above, scald in boiling water for 2–3 min. This shrinks the fruit so that the jar can be tightly filled, with no air-spaces and little or no added liquid. A mixed pack of alternate layers of apples (solid pack) and blackberries (unscalded) is recommended.

Apricots Choose fully ripe fruit, not too soft. Stalk and rinse. Pack whole, *or* halve by slitting and twisting the fruit; stone and pack quickly to avoid browning. A few cracked kernels can be added to each jar.

Blackberries Choose large juicy, fully ripe berries. Remove stalks, leaves and unsound fruit.

Cherries Choose Morello if you can. Should have small stones and plump flesh. Stalk and rinse. Can be stoned, but take care not to lose the juice.

Currants (Black, Red, White) Choose large, firm, juicy and well-flavoured currants. They should be evenly ripened and unbroken. Remove stalks, rinse. Red and white currants have large seeds and are best mixed with raspberries.

Damsons Choose ripe, firm, purple fruit. Stalk and rinse.

Greengages Choose firm, ripe fruit. Remove stalks. After processing, the fruit will turn greenish-brown and the syrup may be cloudy. But if a pressure cooker is used the fruit should keep a good colour due to the short cooking time.

Gooseberries Choose green, hard and unripe berries. Top and tail and, if preserving in syrup, cut off a small slice at either end with a stainless steel knife (this prevents shrivelling and toughening; it is not necessary when preserving in a pressure cooker).

Peaches Choose a free-stone variety (e.g. Hale) just fully ripe. Halve and stone by slitting and twisting the fruit. Dip in a pan of boiling water for 1 min, then put into cold water: the skin should then peel off easily. Pack quickly.

Pears Choose one of the best dessert varieties, e.g. Williams' Bon Chrétien, Conference, Doyenné du Comice, just fully ripened. Peel, halve and scoop out cores and fibres with a sharp-pointed teaspoon. Place in an acid brine (4 pt water; 1 oz salt; $\frac{1}{2}$ oz citric acid), keeping below surface with a plate. Rinse when ready for packing. Pack quickly.

Pears—cooking Prepare like the dessert varieties. Then stew till tender in a sugar syrup (4–6 oz sugar to 1 pt water). Drain, pack and cover with the syrup in which they were cooked. Sterilize as for other pears. These cooking pears will be darker in colour than the dessert varieties.

Plums Choose Victoria plums when they are fully grown but still firm and just turning pink. Choose purple varieties before the colour has developed, when still bright red, and yellow ones when they are still firm and lemon-yellow. Remove stalks, and rinse in cold water. Wipe to remove the bloom. Free-stone varieties can be halved, others must be packed whole. Prick whole plums before preserving in a pressure cooker.

Raspberries Choose large, firm, bright red and well-flavoured berries. Pick carefully, putting the fruit gently in shallow baskets to prevent squashing. Remove plugs and damaged fruit. Preserve as soon as possible; it is not usually necessary to rinse the fruit first.

Rhubarb Choose Champagne or Linnaeus rhubarb and bottle it in the spring when it is tender and needs no peeling. Wipe the stalks and cut in short lengths. Pack straight away (in water or syrup) *or* after soaking. *To soak* pour a hot syrup (8 oz sugar to 1 pt water) over the prepared rhubarb. Leave to soak and shrink for 8–12 hr. Pack, cover with the syrup.

To avoid a white deposit (unsightly but harmless) use previously boiled or softened water.

Bottled gooseberries and gooseberry jam.

Strawberries Hull the berries. Rinse fruit in cold water.

Tight Pack for small soft fruit, e.g. elderberries, blackberries, raspberries, strawberries, mulberries: roll the fruit in castor sugar, then pack into the jars tightly, without any added liquid. Process by either Deep Pan method.

Tomatoes in their own juice: Dip into boiling water for up to 30 seconds (according to ripeness) then into cold water; the skins should then peel off easily. Leave whole, or pack in halves or quarters if large. Press tightly into the jars, sprinkling the layers with sugar and salt—use 1 teasp sugar and 2 teasp salt to each 2 lb tomatoes. No additional liquid is either needed or desirable.

Whole, unskinned tomatoes Remove stalks, rinse tomatoes and pack into jars. Use a brine ($\frac{1}{2}$ oz salt to 1 qt water) in place of syrup or water.

Quick Deep Pan Method

1 Pack prepared fruit tightly into tested jars. Put rubber rings to soak in warm water.

2 Fill jars to overflowing with hot (about 60°C, 140°F) syrup or water. For tomatoes use hot brine.

3 Dip the rubber rings in boiling water and put them on the jars, with the lids. Fasten with screwbands, clips or other grips.

4 If using screwbands, tighten them, then un-screw $\frac{1}{4}$ turn to allow for expansion.

5 Stand jars in the pan on wooden slats or on a thick piece of towelling or cardboard. See that they do not touch each other or the side of the pan. Cover completely with warm (about 38°C, 100°F) water. Put on the lid of the pan.

6 Bring up to simmering point (100°C, 190°F) in 25–30 min. Simmer for time indicated below. Then remove jars one at a time on to a wooden surface (use tongs to lift jars *or*, using a cup, empty out sufficient water to enable you to lift the jars with a cloth).

7 Tighten screwbands. Cool for 24 hr, tightening screwbands further if necessary. Clips should hold properly without attention.

8 Next day, remove screwband or clip. Lift each jar by lid. If properly sealed the lid will stay on securely. Label with date and other details and store in a cool, dark, dry place. Wash, dry

Bottled spiced pears and peaches.

and grease screwbands and clips and store till next year.

Processing times Simmer for time indicated below:

2 min Apple Rings, Blackberries, Currants (Black, Red, White), Gooseberries (for pies), Raspberries, Rhubarb (for pies), Strawberries.

10 min Apricots, Cherries, Damsons, Gooseberries (for dessert), Greengages, Plums (whole), Rhubarb (for dessert), Tight pack of soft Fruit (except Strawberries).

20 min Apples (solid pack), Nectarines, Peaches, Pineapples, Plums (halved), Tight pack of Strawberries.

40 min Pears, Tomatoes (whole).

50 min Tomatoes (in own juice).

Slow Deep Pan Method

This is the same as the quick deep pan method, with the following exceptions:

At step 2, the jars are filled with cold syrup, water or brine.

At step 5, the fastened jars are covered with cold water.

At step 6, the water is raised gradually (i.e. in 90 min) to the temperature indicated below, and kept at that temperature for the time stated.

Processing times *Raise to 70°C, 165°F and maintain at that temperature for 10 min.*

Apple rings, Blackberries, Currants (Black, Red, White), Gooseberries (for pies), Loganberries, Mulberries, Raspberries, Rhubarb (for pies), Strawberries, Whortleberries.

Raise to 80°C, 180°F and maintain at that temperature for 15 min.

Apples (solid pack), Apricots, Cherries, Damsons, Gooseberries (for dessert), Greengages, Nectarines, Plums (whole or halved), Peaches, Pineapples, Rhubarb (for dessert). Tight pack of soft Fruit.

Raise to 100°C, 190°F and maintain at that temperature for 30 min. .

Pears, Tomatoes (whole).

Raise to 100°C, 190°F and maintain at that temperature for 40 min.
Tomatoes (in their own juice).

Bottling Pulped or Puréed Fruit and Tomato Juice

Pulped Fruit Soft and stone fruit, e.g. blackcurrants, apples, tomatoes, plums. Do not use copper or iron utensils. Remove fruit skins if necessary, and any stems and diseased or bruised portions. Peel and core apples. Stone plums. Stew any fruit with just sufficient water to prevent burning. When cooked right through, pour quickly (while still boiling) into hot, clean preserving jars. Seal immediately with hot lids and rubber rings dipped in boiling water. Process, using a pan with a false bottom or lined with a cloth.

To process Cover the jars with hot water, raise to boiling-point and boil for 5 min. Remove from water. Test for seal next day.

Apple purée Cut unpeeled apples into slices, removing bruised or diseased portions. Stew apples till soft in just sufficient water to prevent burning. Rub through a sieve. Add a paring of lemon rind and sugar to taste. Immediately return the pulp and rind to the pan, bring to the boil, stirring to dissolve the sugar, pour into hot preserving jars and seal at once. Process as for pulp above.

Tomato purée Rinse the ripe tomatoes. Heat in a covered pan with a little salt and water. When soft, rub through a hair or nylon sieve. Reheat, and fill quickly into hot preserving jars. Fasten and process, using a pan with a false bottom or lined with a cloth.

To process Cover the jars with hot water, raise to boiling-point, and boil for 10 min. Remove from water. Test for seal next day.

Tomato juice Rinse and heat the ripe tomatoes in a covered pan till they are soft. Sieve through a hair or nylon sieve. To each quart of pulp add: $\frac{1}{2}$ pt water, 1 teasp salt, 1 oz sugar and a pinch of pepper. Re-heat, fasten and process as for Tomato Purée above.

PRESSURE-COOKER BOTTLING

(These instructions apply to most suitable sized pressure pans with a gauge or weight control to maintain a steady pressure. But as different makes of pressure pan vary, consult also the manufacturer's handbook for your particular make.)

1 Place clean, warm, tested preserving jars into a large bowl of very hot water.

2 Remove jars one at a time and pack tightly to the top with prepared fruit. Fill with boiling syrup or water to within $\frac{1}{4}$ in of the top.

3 Dip the rubber rings in boiling water and put them on the jars with the lids. Fasten with screwbands, clips or grips. *If using screwbands, tighten them*, then uncrew them $\frac{1}{4}$ *turn to allow for expansion.* Put jars back into the bowl of hot water until all are packed and fastened.

4 Meanwhile, put the trivet (inverted) and about $1\frac{1}{2}$ pt water into the pressure pan (water should be 1 in deep in the pan). Add 1 tablesp of vinegar or a little lemon juice to prevent the pan from staining. Bring to the boil.

5 Lift the prepared jars of fruit on to the trivet, making sure they do not touch each other or the sides of the pan.

6 Fix on the lid. Allow steam to escape from the centre vent until it will form drops of moisture on a knife blade passed through it.

7 Bring up to 5 lb pressure, adjusting the heat so that it takes about 3 min to bring to pressure (i.e. on a medium heat if using an electric cooker).

8 Process according to the times given below. Lower the heat sufficiently at this stage to maintain a steady pressure. Fluctuations in pressure must be avoided because they cause loss of liquid from the jars and the fruit may be underprocessed.

9 Remove the pan gently away from the heat. *Allow the pressure to drop at room temperature for 10 min.*

10 Lift out the jars one at a time on to a wooden surface, tightening screwbands immediately. Cool 24 hr, tightening screwbands further if necessary. Clips should hold properly without attention.

Dried and candied fruit, and whole fruit preserves.

11 Test, label and store—see Step 8, 'Quick Deep Pan Method'.

Processing times using a pressure pan

Process at 5 lb pressure for 1 min.
Apples (quarters), Apricots, Cherries, Currants (Black, Red, White), Damsons, Fruit Pulp, Fruit Salad, Gooseberries, Plums, Rhubarb (not soaked).
Process at 5 lb pressure for 3 min.
Blackberries, Greengages, Loganberries, Raspberries, Strawberries.
Process at 5 lb pressure for 3–4 min.
Peaches, Pineapples.
Process at 5 lb pressure for 5 min.
Pears, Tomatoes (whole or halved).
Process at 5 lb pressure for 15 min.
Tomatoes (solid pack).

Special preparations for bottling by pressure pan

(a) Soft fruit, e.g. Blackberries, Loganberries, Raspberries, Strawberries.
1 Lay the prepared fruit in a single layer in the bottom of a large enamel, glass or china bowl (not metal).
2 Prepare a syrup with 6 oz sugar to 1 pt water and pour, boiling, over the fruit. Leave to soak overnight.
3 Next morning, drain off the syrup (using this syrup to cover the fruit in the jars). Continue as from No. 1 of the directions for pressure-cooker bottling. The pressure cooking time for a solid pack of soft fruit like this is *3 min at 5 lb pressure.*
(b) Fruit pulp e.g. Apples, Cranberries, Tomatoes.
1 Wash and cut up, without coring or peeling.
2 Remove the trivet from the pressure pan, and pressure cook the fruit or tomatoes in $\frac{1}{4}$ pt water at 15 lb pressure for 2–3 min. (NOTE: The pan must not be more than half full.)
3 Reduce pressure at room temperature. Sieve.
4 *While still hot* (re-heat if necessary), pour into

the prepared warm jars, leaving 1 in headspace.

5 Continue from no. 3–7 of the directions at the beginning of this section.

6 Process at *5 lb pressure for 1 min* and continue with the directions.

(c) Fruit salad Any fruit may be used, but care should be taken not to use too large a proportion of red fruits, such as raspberries, blackcurrants, cherries, etc., or the syrup will be so dark in colour that it will spoil the appearance of fruits such as apricots, gooseberries, greengages, peaches, pears, pineapples.

Each fruit should be prepared in the usual way and the general instructions for bottling by pressure cooker should be followed. But as *only 1 min at 5 lb pressure* is necessary for processing, if hard fruits (such as pineapples or cooking pears) are. used, they should be pre-cooked for 7 min under pressure.

A good syrup should be used for the bottling—at least 8 oz sugar to 1 pt water to allow for the less sweet fruits which may be included.

Oven method

In the time-honoured Oven Method, the fruit is packed into the jars, cooked in the oven, and then removed and boiling liquid added; but the dry heat of the oven causes the fruit to shrink. The Moderate Oven Method given below is a newer and more successful adaptation.

1 Fill the warmed jars with the prepared fruit.

2 Fill to within 1 in of the top with boiling syrup or water.

3 Put on the rubber rings and lids (both first dipped in boiling water). Both clips and screw-bands should not be put on until after the processing.

4 Line a baking-sheet with newspaper, to catch any liquid should it boil over during heating. Stand the jars, 2 in apart, on the paper.

5 Put in the central part of the oven, pre-heated for 15 min, to 150 °C, 300 °F. Process for the times given below.

6 Remove on to a wooden surface. Fasten clips and screwbands and tighten screwbands further

as the jars cool. Next day, test for set (see Step 8, 'Quick Deep Pan Method'), label and store.
Note: Four 1 lb jars require the same processing time as two 2 lb jars.

Processing times using a moderate oven

30–40 min (if processing 1–4 lb)
45–60 min (if processing 5–10 lb)
Apple rings, Blackberries, Currants (Red, Black, White), Gooseberries (for pies), Loganberries, Mulberries, Raspberries, Rhubarb (for pies), Whortleberries.
40–50 min (if processing 1–4 lb)
55–70 min (if processing 5–10 lb)
Apricots, Cherries, Damsons, Gooseberries (for dessert), Greengages, Plums (whole), Rhubarb (for dessert).
50–60 min (if processing 1–4 lb)
65–80 min (if processing 5–10 lb)
Apples (solid pack), Nectarines, Peaches, Pineapples, Plums (halved).
60–70 min (if processing 1–4 lb)
75–90 min (if processing 5–10 lb)
Pears, Tomatoes (whole).
70–80 min (if processing 1–4 lb)
85–100 min (if processing 5–10 lb)
Tomatoes (in own juice).

DRYING AND SALTING
Drying—points to note

1 Use fresh fruits and young, tender vegetables. They usually need to be dried on trays. Special trays can be bought or they can be improvised, e.g. by covering a wire cake rack or oven rack with a loose piece of muslin.

2 In good weather it is sometimes possible to dry fruits and vegetables in the sunshine or in a current of warm air by an open window. But it is generally better to rely on artificial heat, using a temperature of 50°–65°C, 120°–150°F. A cool oven can be used, or—on several successive days—the residual heat from the oven; alternatively,

use a rack over a hot water cistern, or a rack over a coal range, provided there is some protection from the dust.

3 The drying can either take several hours or, if intermittent, 2 or 3 days.

4 It is important to heat very slowly at first to prevent the outside of fruit from hardening or skins from bursting.

5 To store dried fruit and vegetables: leave for

Peaches and pears in brandy – a dessert for a special occasion.

12 hr to cool at ordinary room temperature, then pack in wooden or cardboard boxes lined with greaseproof paper. Keep in a dry place.

DRIED APPLE RINGS

Peel and core the apples and, after removing all blemishes, cut into rings $\frac{1}{4}$ in thick. Place immediately into salt water (2 oz. salt to 1 gal water). After a few minutes, shake off superfluous water and thread the rings on sticks. Balance them across a baking-tin and put to dry at a temperature of not more than 60 °C, 140 °F. If they are dried in continuous heat this may take about 6 hr. When they are dry enough, they should resemble chamois leather in texture. If the centre is pressed with the thumb-nail it should resist the pressure and no juice should ooze out of the apple ring.

DRIED PLUMS

Use a dark-skinned, fleshy variety, e.g. Pond's Seedling. Wash, if necessary, halve and stone, then put to dry. The temperature must be low at first (50 °C, 120 °F) till the skins begin to shrivel. It can then be raised gradually to 65 °C, 150 °F. When it is dry enough, gentle squeezing will not break the skin of the plum or squeeze out any juice from it.

DRIED MUSHROOMS

Use fresh-picked mushrooms. Remove the stems. If the skins are clean and white, it is not necessary to peel the mushrooms. Spread them on trays to dry. Alternatively, thread them on a string, tying a knot between each, and hang up to dry, in a temperature not more than 50 °C, 120 °F, until they are crisp.

DRIED PARSLEY

Wash the parsley and dry in a cloth to remove surplus moisture. Spread on muslin on an oven shelf or tray. Put at the top of a hot oven (230 °C, 450 °F) until dried—about 1 min. Crush between the fingers, then sieve to a coarse powder.

DRIED THYME AND SAGE

Wash, shake the herbs and dry in a cloth to remove surplus moisture. Put the bunches on paper in a warm place. As soon as the leaves can be shaken off the stalks, remove them all and store the thyme in a jar with a tight-fitting lid.

Note: Sage takes longer to dry than thyme and needs to be rubbed through the fingers and sieved.

DRIED MINT AND OTHER HERBS

Wash and dry on a cloth to remove surplus moisture. Tie in a bundle, then put into a paper bag, binding the top of the bag with string so that the herbs are encased with only the stalks projecting. The paper protects them from dust. Hang in a warm place to dry.

SALTING BEANS

Choose fresh, young, tender French beans or runner beans. Wash and dry them and top-and-tail to remove strings. Slice runner beans but leave French beans whole. To every 3 lb beans weigh out 1 lb kitchen salt—not free-running salt. (Weigh accurately and do not use less than this quantity otherwise the beans will become slimy and will not keep.) Pack the salt and beans into a large glass or stoneware jar in the following manner: pack a layer of salt into the bottom of the jar; on top of this, press down very firmly a layer of beans; add another layer of salt, another layer of beans, and continue until the jar is full, finishing with a layer of salt, each layer to be about $\frac{1}{2}$ in thick. Cover, and leave for 3 or 4 days. At the end of this time, you will find that the salt is drawing moisture from the beans and forming a brine, and that there will be room to fill up with more beans and salt, again pressing down very firmly and finishing with a layer of salt. When full to the top, cover the jar securely with several layers of greaseproof paper.

To cook salted beans: Take out as many as required, wash them thoroughly in cold water, then soak them for a couple of hours in warm water—don't soak them overnight or they will toughen. Boil in unsalted water till tender.

Whole Fruit Preserves and Mincemeats

WHOLE-FRUIT PRESERVES

APPLES IN WINE

8 lemons	5 lb apples
1 pt white wine	2 tablesp brandy
4½ lb sugar	

Peel the lemons thinly and pour on 1 pt of boiling water, together with the wine. Leave this to stand for 30 min, then put the mixture into a pan with the juice of the lemons and the sugar. Boil for 10 min. Strain and return to the pan. Peel and core the apples, and cut them into slices. Simmer until they are soft and the syrup is thick. Stir in the brandy. Reheat and pour into hot screw-top jars. This is good served with cream.

Variation

Apple and Cherry Preserve Make as above, but substitute 2 oranges for 2 of the lemons, and 2 lb stoned red cherries for 2 lb apples.

APRICOTS IN GIN

8 oz dried apricots	¼ pt cold water
1 pt boiling water	12 tablesp gin
1 pt granulated sugar	

Pour the boiling water over the apricots and leave them to soak overnight. Drain the fruit, and chop the apricots roughly. Dissolve the sugar in the cold water over gentle heat. Add the apricots and bring the mixture to the boil. Simmer for 15 min. Leave until cold (about 2 hrs). Stir in the gin and store in screw-top jars. This is a good filling for cakes or tarts, or it can be used for pouring over ices or puddings.

Yield—1½ lb

PEACHES IN BRANDY

Peaches	Water
Sugar	Brandy

Dip peaches in hot water, one at a time, and rub off the 'fur' with clean towel. Weigh. For each lb fruit allow ¾ lb sugar and 8 oz (in a measuring jug) water. Boil the sugar and water together for 10 min without stirring. Add the peaches to the syrup and cook (only a few at a time to prevent bruising) for about 5 min until tender. Remove the peaches from the syrup with a strainer and pack firmly into hot sterilized jars. Continue cooking the syrup, after removing peaches, until thick. Cool and measure. Add equal quantity of brandy. Bring to boiling point and fill jars of peaches to overflowing. Seal.

64

Mincemeat.

PEARS AND CHERRIES IN WHITE PORT

1 pt white port OR white wine	4 lb pears, peeled, cored and halved
2 lb sugar	
1 pt water	A little yellow OR orange colouring
Piece of cinnamon stick	
1 lb Morello cherries	

Bring the port, sugar, water and cinnamon stick to the boil. Add the cherries (unstoned) and simmer until the syrup is thick and the cherries almost tender. Add the pear halves and bring the syrup to the boil once more. Simmer for 2–3 min, but do not allow the pears to soften. Pour immediately into sterilized jars, until syrup is about to overflow, and seal.

PLUM CONSERVE WITH JAM

3 lb plums	3½ lb sugar
8 tablesp lemon juice	4 tablesp dark rum

Cut the plums into small pieces and put them into a pan with the lemon juice and sugar. Bring to the boil and boil hard for 3 min, stirring all the time. Add the rum, and leave

65

the mixture to stand for 5 min, stirring often. Put into hot jars and cover.

HONEY FRUIT COMPOTE

½ lb dried prunes	1 pt water
½ lb dried apricots	10 oz clear honey
½ lb dried figs	Thinly pared rind
½ lb dried peaches	of 1 lemon

Soak the dried fruits for 8 hr. Drain. Dissolve the honey in the water and boil, together with the rind, for 5 min. Remove the rind. Pack the fruits into sterilized preserving jars. Cover with syrup to within ½ in of the top of the jars. Stand the jars on a rack in a deep preserving pan and add warm water to come level with the neck of the jars. Bring to the boil and boil for 3 min to expel the air from the jars. Cover with the lids, and screw down to seal. Continue boiling for 25 min. Remove jars to a cooling rack to cool. Label and store.

RAISINS IN RUM

8 oz castor sugar
¼ pt water
8 oz seedless
  raisins
6 tablesp rum

Stir the sugar into the water and bring the mixture gently to the boil. Stir all the time. Add the raisins and simmer for 15 min. Leave about 2 hr until cold. Stir in the rum and store in screw-top jars. This is a good preserve to use on ices, or on hot or cold puddings.

Yield—1 lb

MINCEMEATS

Originally, mincemeat was made with minced meat mixed with dried fruit and spices. Today's mincemeat contains beef suet (a reminder of the traditional meat), apples, dried fruit and spice moistened with spirits which improve both the flavour and keeping quality. Mincemeat should remain fresh and juicy for several weeks, and is better if left to mature for a week or two before using. If the mixture is a little dry, extra spirits can be stirred in before the mincemeat is used. Mincemeat is best packed into clean, dry cold jars, with a cover of brown or greaseproof paper or a plastic top to prevent evaporation and drying out.

MINCEMEAT

1¼ lb cooking apples (prepared weight)	1 level teasp ground nutmeg
1 lb currants	¼ level teasp ground cloves
1 lb seedless raisins	¼ level teasp ground cinnamon
½ lb sultanas	½ level teasp salt
¼ lb candied peel	⅛ pt brandy (SEE note below)
1 lb beef suet	
1 lb sugar	
Grated rind and juice of 2 lemons OR 1 orange and 1 lemon	

Peel and core the apples. Put these with the fruit, candied peel and suet through the mincer. Add the other ingredients and mix well. Cover in jars and use as required.
Note: If the mincemeat is to be used within a few days the brandy may be omitted.

CIDER MINCEMEAT

12 oz cooking
  apples
12 oz raisins
6 oz currants
6 oz soft brown
  sugar
2 teasp ground
  cinnamon
1 teasp ground
  cloves
1 teasp ground
  nutmeg
3 fluid oz cider
1 lemon
3 oz butter

This mincemeat has no suet and will not keep long. It has, however, a delicious flavour, and is worth making at the last minute. Chop the apples and the raisins and put them into a pan with all the other ingredients, including the grated rind and juice of the lemon. Simmer for 30 min. Moisten with a little brandy if necessary. Pack into jars and cover when cold.

COOKED MINCEMEAT

¾ pt apple juice	1 lb chopped
1 lb seedless	mixed peel
raisins	½ teasp ground
1 lb currants	mace
1 lb shredded	1½ teasp
suet	cinnamon
1½ lb soft brown	3 fluid oz brandy
sugar	
6 lb cooking	
apples	

To make the apple juice, mince a large quantity of apples and squeeze them through muslin to get a clear juice. Put the juice in a large pan and bring it rapidly to the boil. Add all the other ingredients except the brandy. Simmer slowly for 1 hr. Stir in the brandy and put into sterilized preserving jars. This mincemeat will keep for 1 year.

LEMON MINCEMEAT

3 large lemons	1 lb shredded suet
3 large cooking	4 oz chopped
apples	mixed peel
1 lb stoned	2 tablesp bitter
raisins	orange marmalade
8 oz currants	5 fluid oz brandy

Grate the rinds of the lemons, and squeeze out the juice. Remove the pith from the lemon peel, and then boil the peel until very tender. Put the peel through the mincer. Bake the apples, remove their skins, and mash the apple pulp. Mix with the lemon peel, dried fruit, sugar, suet, chopped peel, marmalade, brandy, and lemon rind and juice. Put into jars and cover well. Keep for 2 weeks before using.

SHORT-KEEPING MINCEMEAT

8 oz cooking
apples
8 oz currants
8 oz raisins
4 oz chopped
mixed peel
4 oz Demerara
sugar
8 oz white grapes
Grated rind of 1
orange
Grated rind of 1
lemon
1 tablesp lemon
juice
1 teasp mixed
spice
Pinch of salt

As this mincemeat contains no suet, it will only keep for a week in a cool place, but it can be made when supplies run low. Peel and core the apples and cut them into small pieces. Mix with the currants, raisins and peel, and with the sugar. Peel and stone the grapes and chop them roughly. Mix with the orange and lemon rinds and juice, mixed spice and salt. Put into pots and cover well. Store in a cold place.

Pickles, Chutneys and Ketchups

You can often save money by cutting up mis-shapen vegetables and fruits for pickles, chutneys and sauces. But they should be fresh, not over-ripe or in poor condition.

MAKING PICKLES

1 When making vegetable pickles, either soak the vegetables in brine or cover them with layers of salt. This draws out some of the water. When they are covered with spiced vinegar, they should be covered by at least $\frac{1}{2}$ in and the jars should be covered tightly so that none of the vegetables are left uncovered by subsequent evaporation.

2 When making chutneys, make a trial batch first because tastes vary and it may be necessary to adjust the spices in the recipe. But remember when tasting that chutneys are always spicier when first made: they mellow on keeping.

3 Use aluminium or unchipped enamel-lined pans, not brass, copper or iron.

4 If sieving is necessary, use a hair or nylon sieve, since a metal one may give an unpleasant taste.

5 Cover the jars with one of the following:

(a) A cork, boiled to be thoroughly clean, and covered with greaseproof paper.

(b) Synthetic skin.

(c) A well-lacquered metal cap, lined with a layer of cork, waxed cardboard or vinegar-proof paper. The vinegar must not come in contact

69

Fruit bottled in wine.

with the metal otherwise it may cause corrosion and rusting.

(d) Greaseproof paper, covered with a circle of cotton material dipped in melted paraffin wax.

Spiced pickling vinegar

Buy only the best bottled vinegar for pickling; it should have an acetic acid content of at least 5 per cent. It is false economy to buy cheap barrelled vinegar: if—as is often the case—the percentage of acetic acid is too low the pickles will not keep.

For exhibition, white vinegar is often recommended because it shows off the colour and texture of the pickle, but for home use the flavour of malt vinegar is usually preferred.

To make spiced vinegar, add to 1 qt of vinegar: $\frac{1}{2}$ oz cloves, $\frac{1}{2}$ oz allspice, $\frac{1}{2}$ oz ginger, $\frac{1}{2}$ oz cinnamon, $\frac{1}{2}$ oz white pepper.

Note: All these spices should be whole, not ground. Buy them fresh. If you find this spice too strong, reduce the quantities.

Steep the spices in the unheated vinegar for 1–2 months. Shake the bottle occasionally. Then strain and re-cork the bottle until needed.

Quick method If the spiced vinegar is wanted immediately, put the spices and vinegar into a basin. Bring the basin with a plate and stand it in a saucepan of cold water. Bring the water to the boil, remove the pan from the heat, and allow the spices to remain in the warm vinegar for about 2 hr. Keep the plate on top of the basin so that no flavour is lost. Strain the vinegar and use, either cold or hot according to the recipe.

Tarragon vinegar This can be bought ready-made, but if you grow tarragon it is cheaper to make the vinegar at home. Pick the leaves just before the herb flowers. Half-fill a wide-mouthed jar or bottle with the freshly gathered leaves (bang them lightly to bruise them). Fill the jar with best quality malt vinegar and cover. Leave for 2 weeks or longer before removing the leaves. Put a cork or stopper on the jar before storing.

PICKLED APPLES AND ONIONS

Equal quantities of onions and sour apples	½ oz salt to every 2 pt spiced vinegar
Spiced vinegar	

Slice the peeled onions and the peeled, cored apples. Mix well together and fill into jars. Pour on sufficient hot salted spiced vinegar to cover. Seal. This pickle is ready to use when cold.

PICKLED BEETROOT

Beetroots are obtainable most of the year and, like all the root crops, require cooking before pickling. Wash off any soil still clinging to the roots, taking care not to break the skin, for beetroot bleeds easily. If pickling for immediate use, simmer for 1½–2 hr. When cold, skin and cut into squares or slices, and cover with unspiced or spiced vinegar, whichever is preferred.

If pickling for storage, bake the roots in a moderate oven (180°C, 350°F, Gas 4) until tender and, when cold, skin and cut into squares—it packs better that way for keeping; cover with spiced vinegar to which has been added ½ oz salt to each pint.

Beetroot contains a good deal of sugar, and fermentation is more likely than with other vegetables, so seal thoroughly to exclude air.

PICKLED CAULIFLOWER

Cauliflower must not be too mature for pickling, and close-packed heads are best. Break into even-sized pieces, but don't use a knife at all (the stalk of cauliflower stains easily, and this is less likely to occur when broken and not cut). Steep in a brine (½ lb salt to 3 pt water) for 24 hr, drain really well, pack into jars and cover with cold spiced vinegar. If pickling for use later in other mixed pickles, unspiced vinegar can be used for the temporary pickling.

As a straight pickle, cauliflower is best sweet, and sweetening can most easily be done by adding anything from 1 teasp to 1 tablesp sugar (according to size of jar) a couple of days before the pickle is wanted.

Turn the jar up 2–3 times till the sugar is dissolved.

This is much simpler than putting down in a sweet pickle and less likely to develop fermentation.

PICKLED CUCUMBER

The easiest way to pickle cucumbers is to quarter them lengthways, cut into smaller pieces, brine with dry salt for 24 hr, then pack and cover with spiced vinegar. Like most vegetables they are best mixed with others.

PICKLED EGGS

For every 6 eggs allow 1 pt of white wine or cider vinegar, 6 cloves of garlic, 1 oz pickling spice, a small piece of orange peel and a piece of whole mace. Boil together all the ingredients (except the eggs) for ½ hr. When the liquid is cool, strain into a wide-mouthed earthen or glass jar with a screw lid, or tight cork. Put the whole, shelled eggs that have been hard boiled, into the liquid. They can be added to as convenient, but must always be covered by the liquid. The eggs should be left for 6 weeks before eating.

PICKLED GHERKINS

The small immature cucumbers that are known as dills or gherkins require a longer process, especially if their deep green colour is to be fixed. They need partial cooking.

Select gherkins of a uniform size, place in a saucepan and cover with standard brine (½ lb salt to 3 pt water). Bring to near boiling-point; do not actually boil, but simmer for 10 min. Drain until cold, then pack into jars and cover with spiced vinegar, preferably aromatic.

A great many people prefer gherkins sweet; they are particularly popular at cocktail parties. These are quite easy to prepare from the ordinary pickled fruit.

A spoonful of sugar added to the jar and shaken up, then allowed to stand for 24 hr, is all that is needed. Do not do this too long in advance as sugar added to a cold pickle in this way may very easily start to ferment. Another way is to turn the gherkins out on to a shallow dish, the one in which they will be

Mixed pickles.

served, and sprinkle with sugar an hour or two before serving.

PICKLED HORSERADISH

Though this root is obtainable more or less always, it is sometimes an advantage to have a few small jars pickled, if only to avoid digging it up during inclement weather.

Wash the roots in hot water, scrape off the skin, then either grate or put through a mincer. It needs no brining, but add 1 teasp salt to each ½ pt of vinegar used. Pack loosely into small jars and cover with the salted vinegar.

PICKLED LEMONS

No sugar is used and the pickle is very sharp in taste, but is one of the few that goes well with fish.

Select small lemons with thick rinds. Slit them lengthwise in quarters, but don't cut right through. Rub dry salt into these cuts and brine the lemons for 5 days, or until all the salt has melted, turning them in the liquor which forms. Drain off this liquor and add to it enough vinegar to cover the lemons completely, then boil it up with whole pepper and a little ginger. Skim off the scum whilst boiling, allow the pickle to cool and pour it over the fruit, adding to each jar 2 oz mustard seed and 2 cloves of garlic, to every 6 lemons.

Note: Owing to the amount of pepper and mustard, this pickle is very hot and a little goes a long way.

PICKLED MELON, CANTALOUPE AND PUMPKIN

Cantaloupe, pumpkin and melon all belong to the same family and are about 96 per cent water. But each has a distinctive flavour.

Cut in small pieces 8 medium-sized melons. That would about equal 2 pumpkins. Boil 3 qt vinegar with 6 lb sugar and pour over the sliced fruit.

Drain the following morning and bring the liquor to the boil and add 1 oz celery salt, 3 long sticks of cinnamon, 1 tablesp white mustard seed, 20 whole cloves, and 3 pieces of white ginger. When boiling put in the strained fruit, cook slowly for 3 hr, then pack into jars.

PICKLED MUSHROOMS

For pickling, mushrooms need no brining.

Peel them and put them in layers in a pie-dish, sprinkling each layer with salt, 1 teasp to each pound of mushrooms. Cover with spiced vinegar and cook in the oven until they are quite tender, then pack into jars and pour the hot liquor on top. Tie down whilst still hot. Pickled this way they keep well and the liquor is a useful ketchup.

PICKLED NASTURTIUM SEEDS

Nasturtium seeds when pickled are a good substitute for capers, and add variety to salad dressings. They are rather too small to be popular on the table, but go well in clear mixed pickles.

Gather seeds whilst still green on a dry day and steep in brine ($\frac{1}{2}$ lb salt to 3 pt water) for 24 hr. Pack in small jars, warm in the oven for 10 min and cover with hot spiced vinegar. It is best to use a hot spice mixture for these, and a few leaves of tarragon, if available.

The only important thing to remember is to use small jars or bottles, so that they are consumed at once when opened.

Pickled apples and pears.

PICKLED ONIONS

Use small even-sized pickling onions. Peel with a stainless knife and drop them into a basin of salted water until all have been peeled. Remove from water and allow to drain thoroughly before packing into jars or bottles. Cover with cold spiced vinegar and keep for at least 1 month before using.

PICKLED PEACHES

6 lb fresh peaches	3 lb granulated
1 oz cloves	sugar
1 oz allspice	1½ pt distilled
1 oz cinnamon	malt vinegar

Peel the peaches (dipping them first into boiling water then into cold makes peeling easy). Halve, remove the stones and crack some to take out the kernels. Tie the spices in muslin and place with the sugar and vinegar into a pan; bring to the boil to dissolve the sugar. Add the peaches and simmer till just tender but not overcooked or broken. Lift out and pack into clean, warm jars with a few of the blanched kernels. Meanwhile, continue to boil the liquid until it thickens, then pour it over the peaches. Tie down whilst hot and store for at least a week.

PICKLED PEARS

2 lb hard cooking pears	A small piece of root ginger
2 level teasp whole cloves	8 oz sugar
2 level teasp allspice	½ pt vinegar
1 level teasp crushed cinnamon stick	

Crush the spices together and tie in a piece of muslin. Add the muslin bag and the sugar to the vinegar and heat gently until the sugar is dissolved. Peel and core the pears, cut into quarters or eighths and simmer gently in the sweetened spiced vinegar until they are tender but not overcooked or broken. Lift out and pack into clean, warm jars. Meanwhile, continue to boil the vinegar

until it thickens slightly, then pour it over the pears, filling each jar. Tie down and seal securely when cold.
Note: These are best kept for 2–3 months before use.

PICKLED RED CABBAGE

Choose a firm, fresh cabbage. After removing any discoloured outer leaves, cut the cabbage into quarters and then into shreds. Put layers of the shreds into a large basin or dish, sprinkling each layer with salt. Leave overnight. Next day, drain very thoroughly in a colander, pressing out all the surplus liquor.
Pack layers of the shreds into large jars; pack about 3 in of cabbage, cover with a layer of very thinly sliced onion, and sprinkle with 1 teasp brown sugar. Then add another 3 in of cabbage, another layer of onion and another teaspoon of sugar. Continue until the jars are filled, ending with the onion and sugar.
Cover with cold spiced vinegar, tie down and leave for at least 5 days to a week before opening the jar.
Note: Do not make too much of this pickle at a time, because it will lose its essential crispness after 2 or 3 months' storage.

PICKLED SHALLOTS

Use even-sized shallots. Do not skin them; place straight in a brine (1 lb salt to 1 gal water) and leave for 12 hr.
Remove from brine and peel, using a stainless knife. Cover with fresh brine, making sure that all are kept below surface and leave for a further 24–36 hr. Drain thoroughly. Pack tightly in the jars. Cover with cold spiced vinegar so that the vinegar comes ½ in above onions and keep for 3 months before use.

PICKLED WALNUTS

Use walnuts whose shells have not begun to form. Prick well with a silver fork; if the shell can be felt, do not use the walnut. The shell begins to form opposite the stalk, about ¼ in from the end.
Cover with a brine (1 lb salt to 1 gal water) and leave to soak for about 6 days. Drain,

74

make fresh brine, and leave to soak for a further 7 days.

Drain, and spread in a single layer on dishes, leaving exposed to the air, preferably in sunshine, until the nuts blacken (1–2 days). Pack into jars and cover with hot spiced vinegar. Tie down when cold and leave for at least a month before using.

Wear gloves when handling walnuts.

MIXED PICKLES

Make a selection of available vegetables. Any of the following are suitable: small cucumbers, cauliflower, small onions, French beans. Prepare the vegetables: only the onions need be peeled, the rest should merely be cut into suitably sized pieces.

Put all into a large bowl, sprinkle with salt, and leave for 24 hr. Drain thoroughly and pack into jars. Cover with cold spiced vinegar, seal, and leave for at least a month before using.

PICCALILLI

2 lb mixed vegetables
2 oz cooking salt
1 pt vinegar
15 chillies
½ lb granulated sugar
2 oz mustard
½ oz turmeric
2 level tablesp cornflour

Cut into small pieces a variety of vegetables such as cauliflower, cucumber, shallots and young kidney beans, weighing about 2 lb in all when prepared. Place in a large earthenware bowl and sprinkle with the cooking salt. Leave to stand for 24 hr and then drain well. Boil the vinegar and chillies for 2 min, allow to stand for ½ hr and then strain the vinegar.

Mix together the sugar, mustard, turmeric and cornflour. Blend with a little of the cooled vinegar, bring the remainder of the vinegar back to the boil, pour over the blend, return to the saucepan and boil for 3 min. Remove from the heat and fold in the strained vegetables. Pack into prepared jars and cover at once with vinegar-proof covers.

APPLE CHUTNEY

6 lb apples	**3½ lb sugar**
2 lb sultanas	**1 oz salt**
¾ lb preserved ginger	**1 teasp allspice**
3 pt vinegar	

Peel, core and chop the apples into small pieces and chop up the sultanas and ginger. Mix the vinegar, sugar, salt and spice together and bring to the boil, then add the apples and simmer for 10 min before adding the ginger and sultanas. Simmer until the mixture becomes fairly thick, then pour into the jars.

BRISBANE APRICOT AND SULTANA CHUTNEY

1 lb dried apricots
1½ lb onions
1 lb granulated sugar
Grated rind and juice of 2 oranges
½ lb sultanas
1½ pt cider vinegar
1 dessertsp salt
2 cloves garlic, crushed
1 teasp mustard
½ teasp powdered allspice

Soak the apricots overnight, then drain and chop them. Finely chop or mince the onions. Put the apricots and onions in a preserving pan with the sugar, rind and juice of the oranges, the sultanas and the cider vinegar. Add the salt, garlic, mustard and allspice. Simmer until soft, stirring occasionally to prevent sticking. Pour into hot jars, cover and seal.

Yield—5–6 lb

Pickled onions and beetroot.

GOOSEBERRY CHUTNEY

4 lb gooseberries
¼ lb mustard seed
1 lb moist sugar
1 qt vinegar
1 lb onions
1½ lb stoned
  raisins
2 oz allspice
¼ lb salt

Bruise the mustard seed gently. Mix the sugar with 1 pt of the vinegar and boil until a syrup forms, then add the finely chopped onions, raisins and spice.

Boil the gooseberries in the rest of the vinegar until tender, then mix both lots to-

gether and cook until it thickens. Bottle and tie down tightly.

Note: The longer kept the better.

GREEN TOMATO CHUTNEY

5 lb green tomatoes	**1 lb sugar**
1 lb onions	**1 qt vinegar**
½ oz peppercorns	**½ lb raisins**
1 oz salt	**½ lb sultanas**

Slice the tomatoes and chop the onions and mix together in a basin with the peppercorns and salt. Allow this to stand overnight. Next day boil up the sugar in the vinegar, then add the raisins (which may be chopped) and the sultanas. Simmer for 5 min, then add the tomatoes and onions, and simmer till thick.

QUEENSLAND FRUIT CHUTNEY

4 lb apples	2 qt vinegar
2 lb pears	1 level teasp
3 lb tomatoes	cayenne pepper
1 level teasp	1 teasp cloves
mace	1 teasp
½ lb sultanas	peppercorns
½ lb seedless	2 tablesp salt
raisins	1 teasp ground
4 lb sugar	ginger

Peel the apples and pears, core them and cut them into small pieces. Skin the tomatoes and add them to the apples and pears. Add the remainder of the ingredients, and simmer for two hours. Bottle while hot, and seal when cold.

Yield—approx 10 lb

BENTON KETCHUP OR SAUCE

¼ pt vinegar,	1 teasp mixed
preferably wine	mustard
2 tablesp grated	1–2 teasp castor
horseradish	sugar

Bottling Queensland fruit chutney.

77

Mix all the ingredients well together. This sauce will keep for a month. Serve with beef.

TOMATO KETCHUP (1)

6 lb ripe tomatoes	$\frac{1}{2}$ teasp cloves
1 pt vinegar	$\frac{1}{2}$ teap cinnamon
$\frac{1}{2}$ lb sugar	$\frac{1}{2}$ teasp cayenne
1 oz salt	pepper
$\frac{1}{2}$ teasp allspice	

Cut the tomatoes into quarters, place them in a preserving pan with the salt and vinegar and simmer until the tomatoes are quite soft and broken up. Strain the mixture through coarse muslin or a nylon sieve, then return the purée to the preserving pan and add the sugar. Continue to simmer till the ketchup starts to thicken, and then add the spices a little at a time, stirring thoroughly until the flavour is to taste.

When the ketchup is reasonably thick, fill into hot bottles and seal immediately, or allow it to cool slightly, then fill the bottles and sterilize at 80 °C, 170 °F for 30 min. Remember it will be thicker when cold than hot, so don't reduce it too far.

TOMATO KETCHUP (2)

12 ripe tomatoes
2 onions
1 pt vinegar
3 tablesp sugar
1 tablesp salt
2 teasp cloves
2 teasp cinnamon
2 teasp allspice
2 teasp grated
   nutmeg
$\frac{1}{2}$ teasp cayenne
   pepper

Cut the tomatoes into quarters and chop the onions finely. Put all the ingredients into a preserving pan, bring to the boil and cook slowly for 2½ hr. Through very coarse muslin strain out the tomato skins, fill into bottles, sterilize at 77 °C, 170 °F for 30 min, and close whilst hot.

TOMATO KETCHUP (3)

$\frac{1}{4}$ pt malt vinegar	6 oz sugar
1 flat teasp	Pinch of cayenne
pickling spice	pepper
3½ lb tomatoes	$\frac{1}{2}$ oz salt
$\frac{1}{4}$ lb onions, peeled	1 tablesp tarragon
$\frac{1}{2}$ lb apples	vinegar

Bring the pickling spice to the boil with the malt vinegar and leave to infuse for 2 hr before straining. Meanwhile, cut up the tomatoes, onions and apples (the onions should be peeled, but there is no need to peel or core the tomatoes and apples). Simmer these cut-up fruits and vegetables very slowly in a covered pan—the juice from the tomatoes should be sufficient to prevent burning. When they are thoroughly softened, rub through a hair or nylon sieve. Return the pulp to the pan; add the sugar, pepper and salt, and boil—with the lid off the pan—till the sauce begins to thicken, stirring occasionally with a wooden spoon. Add the strained malt vinegar and the tarragon vinegar. Boil—with the lid off the pan—till thick and creamy. Pour into hot bottles and seal. Sterilize in a simmering water bath for 30 min.

PRESSURE-COOKER CHUTNEYS AND SAUCES

APPLE CHUTNEY

3 lb apples
1 lb onions
$\frac{1}{2}$ pt vinegar
1 dessertsp salt
$\frac{1}{4}$ teasp cayenne
   pepper
$\frac{1}{4}$ lb preserved
   ginger
$\frac{1}{2}$ lb sultanas
1½ lb sugar

Peel, core and cut up apples. Peel onions and slice finely. Remove trivet. Put the apples and onions into the pressure cooker, together with vinegar and all ingredients, except sugar. Stir well, cover cooker and bring to 15 lb pressure in usual way. Pressure cook 10 min and allow pressure to reduce at room temperature. Remove cover, add sugar, stir until dissolved, then boil steadily until the chutney is the consistency of thick jam. Pour into hot jars and seal immediately.

GREEN TOMATO CHUTNEY

3 lb green tomatoes	½ oz root ginger
1 lb sour apples	1 teasp salt
¾ lb dates	¼ pt vinegar
¼ lb onions	¼ lb sugar

Skin the tomatoes. Peel and core the apples and cut into very small pieces with the dates. Chop the onions. Tie the ginger in a muslin bag. Remove the trivet from the pressure cooker. Put all the ingredients, except the sugar, into the pressure cooker. Stir well, cover, bring to 15 lb pressure and pressure cook for 10 min. Reduce pressure at room temperature. Add the sugar and simmer with the lid off the cooker until the chutney is of a thick consistency. Remove the ginger. Put the chutney into warm jars and seal.

PLUM CHUTNEY

3 lb plums
2 medium onions
2 medium apples
4 tablesp ground
    ginger
4 tablesp
    cinnamon
4 tablesp allspice
1½ tablesp salt
1 pt vinegar
    (approx)
¾ lb sugar

Peel and chop the onions; peel, core and chop the apples; stone the plums and cut the plums in quarters. Remove the trivet from the pressure cooker. Put into the cooker the plums, onions and apples, the spices and salt and half the vinegar. Bring to the boil slowly in the open cooker, then cover, bring to 15 lb pressure in the usual way, and cook for 10

min. Reduce pressure at room temperature. Return the cooker to the heat and, stirring all the time, add some of the vinegar gradually until the mixture is thick and smooth. Add the sugar and if necessary a little more of the vinegar, then boil rapidly until the chutney is the consistency of thick jam. Pour into hot jars and seal immediately.

RED TOMATO CHUTNEY

2 lb tomatoes
1 apple
1 onion
6 oz sultanas
3 oz dates
3 teasp mixed
    whole spice
1 oz salt
½ pt vinegar
½ lb brown sugar

Skin the tomatoes. Peel, core and slice the apple. Peel and slice the onion. Wash the sultanas and dates in hot water before chopping. Remove the trivet from the pressure cooker, then put in these ingredients. Add the spices, tied in a muslin bag, the salt and ¼ pt of the vinegar. Bring to 15 lb pressure and cook for 10 min. Allow pressure to reduce at room temperature. Add the rest of the vinegar and the sugar and stir until the sugar is dissolved. Bring to the boil and simmer gently, in the open cooker, until thick. Pour into hot jars and seal immediately.

TOMATO SAUCE

6 lb tomatoes	Pinch of cayenne
¼ pt water	pepper
½ teasp ground	1 oz salt
ginger	½ lb sugar
½ teasp ground	1 gill vinegar
mace	
½ teasp ground	
cloves	

Slice the tomatoes; remove the trivet from the pressure cooker and put the tomatoes in the cooker together with the water. Bring to

Ingredients for Benton and tomato ketchup.

15 lb pressure over a medium heat, and pressure cook for 3 min. Reduce pressure immediately with cold water, and rub the pulp through a hair or nylon sieve. Dissolve the spices, salt and sugar in the vinegar and return, together with the sieved tomatoes, to the open cooker. Stir over a medium heat until the consistency of thick cream—this takes ½ hr or longer.

With a pressure cooker, it is easy to sterilize this sauce so that it can be kept.

(a) Pour the sauce immediately into hot, prepared bottling jars, leaving 1 in head space; adjust rings and lids; if using screw-top jars, screw bands tight, unscrewing ¼ turn.

(b) Rinse out the cooker and return it to the stove with 1½ pt boiling water, to which 1 tablesp vinegar has been added, and put in the inverted trivet.

(c) Lift in the prepared jars, and bring cooker to 5 lb pressure over a medium heat. This process should take approximately 5 min.

(d) Pressure cook for 2 min.

(e) Remove the cooker from the heat and reduce pressure at room temperature for 10 min.

(f) Lift out jars; tighten screwbands and leave for 24 hr.

(g) Test seal and store in a cool dark place.

Yield—2 pt

Fruit syrups and Vinegars

USE ONLY SOUND, ripe fruit for this purpose and preferably loaf sugar. The syrup or vinegar when ready must be put into perfectly clean, dry bottles and stored in a cool, dry cellar or cupboard. If it is kept for any considerable time, it should be sterilized. To do this, stand the bottles on a layer of straw in a large pan, without them touching each other or the sides of the pan, with the corks or stoppers loosened; pour warm water into the pan and heat gradually to boiling-point. To prevent touching, the bottles may be wrapped in cloth. After $\frac{1}{2}$ hr lower the heat gradually and when cool lift out the bottles, wipe them and tighten the cork or stoppers; seal if necessary.

APRICOT SYRUP

Sound, ripe
  apricots
Water
Allow 1 lb loaf
  sugar to every
  pt juice

Three-quarters fill a large jar with apricots, stoned and cut in halves, add half the kernels. Stand the jar in a pan of boiling water and simmer until the fruit is quite soft and the juice flows freely. Strain off the liquid through a fine sieve or jelly bag, measure it carefully and add sugar in the proportion stated above. Boil up again for 10 min, removing the scum as it rises. Stand aside and when quite cool pour into clean dry bottles. Pour a little olive oil on the top in each bottle, cork securely and seal with bottling wax.

The oil at the top of each bottle must be carefully removed with a piece of clean cotton wool before use. The syrup is usually diluted with plain or aerated water.

Variations: Substitute cherries, greengages, peaches, plums or rhubarb for apricots.

APRICOT VINEGAR

3 gal sound, ripe apricots	To every qt syrup allow:
To every pt liquid allow:	$\frac{1}{2}$ pt brandy
1 lb loaf sugar	
1 gal white wine vinegar	

Halve the apricots and put them into an earthenware bowl or pan. Pour over them the white wine vinegar. Cover with a clean cloth and let them stand undisturbed for 4 days. Strain off the liquid through a fine sieve or jelly bag, measure carefully and stir in sugar in the proportion stated above. Boil up for 30 min, removing the scum as it rises. Stand aside and when it is quite cool measure the syrup and pour in brandy in the proportion stated above. Bottle, cork securely and seal.

Variations: Substitute cherries, damsons, greengages, peaches, or plums for apricots.

BLACKBERRY or BLACKCURRANT SYRUP

To each lb of fruit allow:

1 lb loaf OR preserving sugar and 1 tablesp water

To each pt syrup allow:

1 small glass brandy

Place the fruit, sugar and water in a large jar with a close-fitting cover, stand the jar in a saucepan of boiling water, and cook gently for 2 hr. Strain the juice, measure it, put it into a preserving pan or stewpan (preferably an enamelled one), and boil gently for 20 min, skimming carefully meanwhile. To each pt of syrup add a small glass of brandy, let it become quite cold, then bottle for use.

BLACKBERRY VINEGAR

6 qt sound, ripe blackberries 4 pt white wine vinegar	1 lb loaf sugar for every pt liquid

Put the fruit in a large earthenware jar and pour over it the white wine vinegar. Cover with a clean cloth and let stand for 4 days. Strain off the liquid through a fine sieve, measure it carefully and add sugar in the pro-

portion stated above. Bring to the boil and cook for 20 min, removing the scum as it rises. Stand aside and when quite cold pour into bottles. Cork and seal the bottles and store them in a cool, dry cupboard.

BLACKCURRANT VINEGAR

4 qt sound, ripe blackcurrants 2 pt picked and washed young currant leaves	Loaf sugar White wine vinegar Brandy

Put the fruit and currant leaves into a preserving pan and crush and stir them over gentle heat until the juice flows freely. Strain the juice off through a fine sieve, measure and add 12 oz sugar for every pt of juice. Bring to the boil and cook for 20 min, removing the scum as it rises. Stand aside until cold, then measure and add 3 gills white wine vinegar for every pt of syrup. Finally add 1 gill of brandy for every qt of liquid. Bottle, cork, seal and store in a cool, dry cupboard.

CRANBERRY SYRUP

12 lb sound ripe cranberries 1 lb loaf sugar to each pt of juice

Crush the fruit in a jar standing in a pan of boiling water. Cook gently for 2 hr. Strain off the liquid through a fine sieve, measure carefully and add sugar in the proportion stated above. Bring to the boil again and cook for 15 min, removing the scum as it rises. Stand aside until quite cold, then pour into bottles. Cork and seal the bottles securely and store in a cool, dry place.

Variations: Substitute gooseberries, raspberries or strawberries for cranberries.

CRANBERRY VINEGAR

6 lb sound, ripe cranberries 3 qt white wine vinegar	1 lb loaf sugar to each pt of liquid

Put the fruit in an earthenware jar, crush it and pour over the vinegar. Cover with a clean cloth and let it stand for 10 days, stirring from time to time. Strain off the liquid through a fine sieve, measure it carefully and add sugar in the proportion stated above. Bring to the boil and cook for 10 min, removing the scum as it rises. Stand aside and when quite cold, bottle. Cork and seal the bottles securely.

Variations: Substitute gooseberries, rhubarb or strawberries for cranberries.

DAMSON SYRUP

Sound ripe damsons	1 lb loaf sugar to each pt of juice

Place the fruit in an earthenware jar, stand it in a pan of boiling water and cook until the juice flows freely. Strain off the juice through a fine sieve, measure it carefully and add sugar in the proportion stated above. Bring to the boil again and cook for 10 min, removing the scum as it rises. Stand aside and when quite cold, bottle. Pour a little olive oil on the top of each bottle, cork and seal. As each bottle is opened the oil must be carefully removed with a piece of clean cotton wool. Dilute the syrup with plain or aerated water.

ELDERETTE

Sound ripe elderberries

To every pt of liquid allow:
1 lb loaf sugar, 4 cloves and ½ in bruised cinnamon stick

To every pt of syrup allow:

1 wineglass brandy

Crush some elderberries and mix the strained juice with an equal quantity of cold water. Add sugar, cloves and cinnamon in the proportion stated above and boil together for 10 min. Then strain and measure the syrup and

stir in brandy in the proportion stated above. Bottle when quite cold and store.

FIG SYRUP

3 lb sound ripe figs	1 lb loaf sugar to
3 pt water	every pt of
3 lemons	liquid

Cut the figs up into slices and put them in an earthenware jar together with the water and the strained juice and thinly peeled rind of the lemons. Stand the jar in a pan of boiling water and cook gently for 3 hr. Strain off the liquid through a fine sieve, measure carefully and stir in sugar in the proportion stated above. Boil up again for 10 min, removing the scum as it rises. Stand aside and, when quite cold, bottle, cork and seal securely. Store in a cool, dry place.

GINGER SYRUP

8 oz bruised ginger	1 lemon
3 pt water	3 lb loaf sugar

Put the ginger into an earthenware jar containing the water. Stand the jar in a pan of boiling water, add the strained juice and the thinly peeled rind of the lemon, and the sugar, and cook for 30 min, removing the scum as it rises. Strain off the liquid through a fine sieve and when quite cold pour into clean, dry bottles. Cork and seal for storage.

LEMON SYRUP

**2 lb loaf sugar
2 pt water
1 oz citric acid
A few drops of lemon essence**

Boil the sugar and water together for 15 min, put the liquid into a basin, and leave to get cold. Beat the citric acid to a powder, mix with it the lemon essence, then add to the syrup, mix well, and bottle for use. Two tablesp of the syrup are sufficient for a tumbler of cold water, and will be found a very refreshing summer drink.

MULBERRY VINEGAR

3 lb sound, ripe mulberries	Allow 2 lb loaf sugar to every
2 qt white wine vinegar	qt of liquid

Put the mulberries into an earthenware jar, crush them and pour over the white wine vinegar. Cover with a clean cloth and let stand for 7 days, stirring from time to time. Strain off the liquid through a fine sieve, measure it carefully and add sugar in the proportion stated above. Bring to the boil and cook for 10 min, removing the scum as it rises. Stand aside and when quite cold, bottle. Cork and seal securely and store in a cool, dry cupboard.

ORGEAT SYRUP

4 oz sweet almonds	1 pt cold water
1 oz bitter almonds	1¼ lb castor sugar
Orange flower water	½ teasp lemon essence

Blanch and pound the almonds with a few drops of orange flower water. Put in an earthenware jar and pour over the cold water. Stir well and add the sugar, lemon essence and 1 tablesp orange flower water. Let the jar stand in a warm place for 6 hr. Bring to the boil and cook for 15 min, then strain off all the liquid, pressing the residue well to extract all the juice. Bottle in the usual way. Dilute with cold water when required for use.

PEAR SYRUP

6 lb sound, ripe juicy pears	To every pt of syrup allow:
1½ pt cold water	A few drops of strawberry essence and 1 wineglass brandy
To every pt of liquid allow:	
12 oz loaf sugar	
2 lemons	

Put the peeled, cored and sliced fruit into an earthenware jar and pour over the cold water. Add the thinly peeled rinds of the lemons and stand the jar in a pan of boiling water. Cook gently for 1 hr. Strain off the liquid through a fine sieve, measure carefully and stir in sugar in the proportion stated above. Bring to the boil again and cook for 15 min, removing the scum as it rises. Stand aside and when quite cold, work in the strawberry essence and the brandy. Bottle, cork securely and seal for storage.

QUINCE SYRUP

Sound, ripe quinces	Loaf sugar

Cut up and mash the fruit and put it into an earthenware jar stood in a pan of boiling water and cook steadily until the fruit is quite soft and the juice flows freely. Strain the liquid off, measure it carefully and stir in loaf sugar, allowing 1 lb sugar to every pt of juice. Bring to the boil and cook for 10 min, removing the scum as it rises. Stand aside and when quite cold, bottle and store in the usual way.

RASPBERRY SYRUP

6 lb sound ripe raspberries	½–¾ lb loaf sugar to each pt of juice

Crush the fruit in a jar standing in a pan of boiling water. Cook gently for about 1 hr to extract all the juice. Strain through a fine nylon sieve. Measure the juice and add the sugar. Bring back to the boil and cook for 15 min, removing the scum as it rises. Let stand until quite cold, then pour into bottles. Lock, seal, store and use as required. Gooseberries, cranberries or strawberries can be used in the same way.

RASPBERRY VINEGAR

2 qt raspberries
2 qt white wine vinegar
1 lb loaf OR preserving sugar to every pt of liquid

Put the raspberries into a wide-necked glass bottle, or an unglazed jar; pour over them the vinegar; cover, and let the liquid stand for 10 days, stirring it once or twice daily.

84

Pears in red sauce.

Strain and measure the vinegar: add sugar in the proportion stated above and stir occasionally till the sugar is dissolved. Pour into a jar, place the jar in a saucepan of boiling water, and simmer gently for $1\frac{1}{4}$ hr, skimming when necessary. When quite cold, rack off into bottles and store in a cool, dry place, for use.

ROSE HIP SYRUP

6 pt water	**2 lb preserving**
3 lb ripe, wild, rose	**sugar**
hips	

Boil 4 pt of the water. Mince the hips coarsely and put immediately into the boiling water. Heat until the water boils again, skim off the scum as it rises and boil for a few minutes. Then allow to cool for about 15 min. Pass the pulp through fine linen or muslin twice to ensure that all the hairs are removed. Put the liquid obtained to one side. Boil the pulp again with the remaining 2 pt water, leave to cool for 15 min, and strain twice as before. Return both extracted liquids to the pan and boil until the juice is reduced to about 3 pt. Sweeten, stirring well. Pour into warmed bottles, seal; store in a dark cupboard until required.

Home-made Wines and Beers

Town dwellers are apt to think that wine-making is only for country people. But wines can be made equally well in cities; you need take only a little trouble to turn the fruits or flowers picked on a day's excursion into the country into wine for future enjoyment. It is wrong to think wine cannot be made in small quantities. It is possible to turn out six or less bottles at a brewing.

HOW TO MAKE WINE

Equipment

One or more (depending on the quantity to be made) large earthenware or enamel bowls capable of holding 2–3 gallons will be required. On no account must metal utensils be used; use a wooden spoon for stirring.

For wine-making on a reasonably large scale—say 5 gallons (about 30 bottles) at a time—a cask and a tub may be preferable. An alternative to a cask is two stone jars of the 'demijohn' type, each holding $2-2\frac{1}{2}$ gallons. Enough wine to fill the receptacle plus a little more to allow for loss by evaporation and sediment must be made. Small quantities of wine can be made without a cask or jar—the wine, after straining, being put direct into the bottles from the fermenting bowl, and the bottles left covered until, when fermentation dies down, they may be corked.

To prepare yeast for wine-making

Fresh yeast is not really necessary nowadays, as there are several kinds of packeted dried yeast on sale. Put a little water in a cup and sprinkle the surface liberally with dried yeast. The yeast is absorbed within $\frac{1}{2}$ hr, after which stir it to a thick paste. Spread it on a piece of dry toast to a thickness of about $\frac{3}{4}$ in. The toast, for a $2\frac{1}{2}$-gallon making, should be a little larger than a playing-card. (Note that double the quantity of wine does not need double the quantity of yeast, about half as much again is roughly the amount required.) The toast should be placed yeast downwards on the surface of the juice in the fermenting vessel.

Fermentation can be rather a tricky process. On tasting the 'must'—as the juice is called during fermentation—after a week or so, it may be found that there is little sweetness in it. This indicates that too much yeast has been added at the beginning, and that it has 'devoured' most of the sugar. More sugar should be added; if the 'must' tastes too sweet, add more yeast.

Step-by-step directions for making wine

1 The fruit for wine-making should be really ripe. Remove stalks and discard any bad fruit.
2 Bring the water to boiling-point and pour over the fruit; this may have to be done in relays if one has not the necessary equipment for boiling large quantities of water. Pulp the fruit either with a wooden spoon or with the hand, after which leave the fruit to stand for a week, stirring it daily.
3 Strain the pulp, using a straining bag of muslin.
4 Put the juice back into the fermenting vessel, add the sugar and yeast (if used).
5 Having dissolved the sugar in the liquid, leave it to ferment. The vessel must be closely covered with some material during this time.

6 After a day or two there should be signs of fermentation on the surface of the 'must' which is now acquiring a scum; remove this scum periodically. Fermentation is detected by tiny bubbles bursting on the scum, and when really under way there is also a faint hissing sound. If after a few days there is no sign of fermentation, it must be induced. Perhaps the surrounding atmosphere is too cold, in which case the vessel should be moved to a warmer spot; or possibly there is a deficiency of sugar.

7 After about a fortnight the fermentation should have died down, when the wine should be finally skimmed and preferably strained again. This second straining *must* be done if yeast has been used.

8 Using an ordinary milk jug transfer the wine to the cask, jar or bottles. Cover with a wad of dampened cloth.

9 As fermentation proceeds a slight hissing will be heard; a certain amount of froth will also be thrown up, most of which will be absorbed by the pad. Rinse out the pad daily to keep it sweet.

10 When all hissing has ceased introduce some finings to help the wine to clear. This is done by melting a little isinglass in a small quantity of wine and heating but not boiling it. A little of this liquid—about 1 teasp to a bottle—is poured gently into the wine, the upper part of which is then vigorously stirred with a stick. The finings will eventually sink slowly through the wine, carrying all suspended matter to the bottom. Gelatine makes a good substitute for isinglass. If brandy is being added it should be added at the time of the fining.

11 Bottle the wine.

Bottling

After the 'must' has been strained at the end of the first fermentation, the wine is still 'alive' so on no account must the corks of bottles or jars, or the bungs of casks be put in tightly, otherwise the bottles may burst or the corks or bungs blow out. It is preferable to place a wad of cloth, which

88

should be kept moistened, over the mouths of the bottles, jars or casks, as in Note 8, and not to put in the corks at all for a week or two.

The process which takes place in the casks, jars or bottles when the wine is transferred from the fermenting vessel is called 'secondary fermentation', during which any sediment will sink to the bottom. At the end of fermentation this must be got rid of.

With casks the tap aperture is usually above the level of the sediment, or 'lees', as it is called; so the wine can be drawn off through the tap, the 'lees' disposed of and the wine returned to the cask. This should now be bunged tightly and the wine allowed to 'rest' for whatever period is stated in the recipe. It is always advisable that there should be a spigot or vent-peg in the bung, which will blow out as a warning should a delayed fermentation take a vigorous turn.

With jars or bottles which have been standing upright, it is almost impossible to pour off the wine without disturbing the lees and thus spoiling a good deal of wine, but the wine can be drawn out by means of a glass syringe with rubber tubing attached, the jars or bottles rinsed, and the wine replaced. The corks cannot be tightly fixed however until certain that the fermentation is complete, perhaps two months later. The corks can then be gently hammered in, cut flush with the bottle, and made airtight with a film of sealing-wax.

APPLE WINE

1 gal mashed apples	Loaf sugar
1 gal boiling water	

Put the mashed apples into a basin and pour over them the boiling water. Cover with a cloth and let stand for 2 weeks. Strain and weigh the liquid and add $\frac{1}{2}$ lb sugar for every 1 lb weight of liquid. Stir until the sugar has dissolved then cover the basin again. Skim off the scum which forms and leave until next day when the liquid will be ready to bottle. Cork and seal carefully.

APRICOT WINE

12 lb sound but not over-ripe apricots	Small quantity of yeast spread on toast
3 gal water	1 pt white wine
1 lb loaf sugar	

Remove the stones of the fruit, take out the kernels, and cut each apricot into 6–8 pieces. Put them into a preserving pan with the water, sugar and about half the kernels, and simmer very gently for 1 hr. Turn into an earthenware vessel, let it remain undisturbed until cool, then put in the yeast on toast.

90

Cover the vessel with a cloth, let it remain undisturbed for 3 days, then strain the liquid into a clean, dry cask, add the white wine, and bung lightly.

At the end of 6 months draw off the wine into bottles, cork them closely, store in a cool, dry place for about 12 months, and the wine will then be ready for use.

Note: Dried apricots may be used but they must be soaked until well swollen before use.

BEETROOT WINE

Allow 4 lb beetroot to every gallon water. Leave them overnight in enough cold water to cover. Then peel, and cut them into slices about 1 in thick. Put them into the water and simmer for about 1 hr, having first added a cupful of hops, several oranges and a lemon cut into quarters, and a few cloves with a piece or two of bruised ginger. (Omit the hops if difficult to obtain.) Strain, and to the liquid left, add sugar in the proportion of 2 lb sugar to each gallon, and simmer until this is dissolved, stirring all the time. Put in the yeast, spread on toast.

Ferment for about 2 weeks, stirring and skimming daily. Strain again and transfer to cask or stone jar and bottle in 2–3 months.

BLACKBERRY WINE

4 gal sound, ripe
   blackberries
4 gal boiling water
Loaf sugar
Cinnamon
Brandy

Crush the blackberries in a large bowl or tub and pour over them the boiling water. Stir well, cover with a cloth and leave undisturbed for 4–5 days. Without breaking up the crust which has formed on the surface, strain off the liquid and measure it carefully. For every gallon of liquid add 1 lb sugar and pour into a clean cask, reserving about a gallon of the liquid to fill up the cask as fermentation ceases. This wine generally clears itself, but the addition of isinglass is recommended. Let it stand for about a fortnight. Then add 1 stick of cinnamon and 1 gill brandy for every gallon of wine, secure

the bung and leave undisturbed for 12 months.

Note: Unless the blackberries are very ripe, double the above sugar will be needed.

BLACKCURRANT WINE

2 gal fresh black-	2 gal cold water
currant juice	Brandy
7 lb loaf sugar	

Put the blackcurrant juice, sugar and water into a clean cask. Let it stand in a warm corner until fermentation ceases. Rack the liquid off, measure, and add 1 pt brandy for every 2–3 gallons of wine. Secure the bung and leave undisturbed for at least 9 months. Bottle and seal and the wine will be ready for use in a year at the outside.

CHAMPAGNE-ENGLISH

3 gal unripe yellow	12 lb loaf sugar
gooseberries	1½ pt gin
3 gal water	½ oz isinglass

Top and tail the gooseberries and put them in a large pan or tub. Crush them and pour over the water. Let them remain for 48 hr, stirring from time to time meanwhile. Crush thoroughly and strain off all the liquid. Stir into this the sugar and let it stand for about 3 days covered by a clean cloth but stirring from time to time. Then strain the liquid into a clean cask, adding the gin and isinglass previously dissolved in a little water. Place the bung in loosely and do not secure until fermentation has ceased.

The wine should stand undisturbed in the cask for 12 months before bottling.

CHERRY WINE

Ripe cherries	Ground allspice
Loaf sugar	Brandy
Ground mace	Rum
Ground cloves	

Stone the cherries, put the cherries into a large jar, place in a saucepan of boiling water, and cook gently until the juice is all extracted. Then strain into a preserving pan, and for each quart of juice add ½ lb sugar, a pinch each of mace, cloves and allspice. Boil and skim until clear. Let it cook, then add ½ pt brandy and ½ pt rum for each quart of juice, pour into bottles, and cork fairly closely at first.

CIDER WINE

4 gal apple juice
4 lb honey
1 oz white tartar
¼ oz cloves
¼ oz mace
¼ oz cinnamon
1 qt Jamaica rum

Place the apple juice, honey and tartar, with the cloves, mace and cinnamon in a clean cask and cover the bung hole with a piece of clean cloth. Let it remain undisturbed until fermentation has ceased. Pour in the rum and fasten the bung securely. The wine will be ready for bottling in 6 months.

COLTSFOOT WINE

12 lb loaf sugar
6 lemons
6 gal water
5 gal freshly gath-
  ered coltsfoot
  flowers
5 lb stoned
  chopped raisins
Yeast
1 qt brandy

Boil the sugar and the strained juice of the lemons in the water for about ½ hr, skimming from time to time as necessary. Place the coltsfoot flowers, raisins and thinly peeled rind of the lemons in a tub or large basin and pour over them the hot liquid. Stir steadily until nearly cold, then stir in the yeast. Cover with a clean cloth and let it stand undisturbed for 3–4 days. Strain off into a clean cask, reserving 2–3 pt of the liquid to fill up the cask as fermentation subsides. Place the bung in lightly until the hissing has ceased, then pour in the brandy and secure the bung

tightly. The wine will be ready for bottling in 6 months' time.

COWSLIP WINE

4 qt cowslip
  flowers
3 lb loaf sugar
4 qt water
1 orange
1 lemon
¼ oz dried yeast
  moistened with
  water
¼ pt brandy
  (optional)

Boil the sugar and water together for ½ hr, skimming when necessary, and pour, quite boiling, over the finely grated rind and strained juice of the orange and lemon. Let it cool, then put in the yeast and cowslip flowers, cover with a cloth, and allow it to remain undisturbed for 48 hr. Strain and pour into a clean, dry cask, add the brandy, bung closely, let it remain for 8 weeks, then draw it off into bottles. Cork securely, store in a cool, dry place for 3–4 weeks, and it will then be ready for use.

DAMSON WINE

Damsons	Loaf sugar
Boiling water	Brandy

Remove the stalks, put the fruit into an earthenware bowl, pour in 1 gallon boiling water for each gallon of damsons, and cover with a cloth. Stir the liquid 3 or 4 times daily for 4 days, then add 4 lb loaf sugar and ½ pt brandy for each gallon of liquor. When the sugar is dissolved, strain into a clean dry cask. Cover the bung-hole with a cloth, folded into several thicknesses, until fermentation ceases, then bung tightly, and allow the cask to remain undisturbed for 12 months in a moderately warm place. At the end of this time it should be racked off into bottles.

The wine may be used at once, but if well corked and stored in a dry place it may be kept for years.

92

DANDELION WINE

4 qt dandelion
   flowers
4 qt boiling water
1 lemon
1 orange
3 lb loaf sugar
1 in whole ginger
$\frac{1}{4}$ oz dried yeast
   moistened with
   water

Put the petals of the flowers into a bowl, pour over them the boiling water, let the bowl remain covered for 3 days, meanwhile frequently stirring it well. Strain the liquid into a preserving pan, add the finely peeled rinds of the lemon and orange, sugar, ginger and the thinly sliced lemon (the white pith should be stripped off and discarded). Boil gently for about $\frac{1}{2}$ hr, and when cool add the yeast spread on a piece of toast. Allow it to stand for 2 days, then turn it into a cask, keep it well bunged down for 8–9 weeks, and bottle the wine for use.

ELDERBERRY WINE

7 lb elderberries	Ground ginger
3 gal water	Cloves
Loaf sugar	Dried yeast
Raisins	Brandy

Strip the berries from the stalks, pour the water, quite boiling, over them, let them stand for 24 hr, then bruise well and drain through a nylon sieve or jelly bag. Measure the juice obtained, put it into a preserving pan and for each gallon of liquid add 3 lb sugar, 1 lb raisins, $\frac{1}{2}$ oz ginger and 6 cloves. Boil gently for 1 hr, skimming when necessary. Let the liquid stand until lukewarm, then put in $\frac{1}{2}$ teasp yeast for each gallon of liquor and turn into a clean, dry cask. Cover the bung-hole with a folded cloth, let the cask remain undisturbed for 14 days, then stir in $\frac{1}{4}$ pt brandy for every gallon of liquor and bung tightly.
In about 6 months the wine may be drawn off into bottles, tightly corked, and stored for use.

ELDERFLOWER WINE

6 gal water	Dried yeast
16 lb loaf sugar	4 large lemons
4 pt elderflowers	$\frac{1}{4}$ pt brandy to
8 lb raisins	each gal of wine

Boil the water and sugar together for 10 min, removing the scum as it rises. Put the elder-flowers into a large basin or tub with the raisins, stoned and cut up into small pieces, and pour the syrup over them. Stir well and when just lukewarm put in the yeast. Cover with a clean cloth and let stand undisturbed until next day. Then add the strained juice and the thinly peeled rind of the lemons. Re-cover and allow to stand for 3 more days. Strain the liquid into a clean cask, reserving a small quantity to fill up with as fermentation subsides. As soon as the hissing has entirely ceased, add brandy in the proportion stated above and tighten the bung. At the end of 6 months it will be ready for bottling.

GINGER WINE

$\frac{1}{4}$ lb raisins	$\frac{1}{4}$ lb whole ginger
3 gal cold water	4 lemons
9 lb loaf sugar	Dried yeast

Stone and halve the raisins, put them into a large preserving pan with the water, sugar and ginger (bruised); boil for 1 hr, skimming frequently. Add the rind of the lemons and turn into a large earthenware bowl or wood-en tub; allow the liquid to stand until luke-warm, then put in the yeast. On the following day put into a clean, dry cask, add the juice of the lemons, and bung lightly. Stir the wine every day for a fortnight, then tighten the bung.
Let the wine remain undisturbed for 3–4 months, when it may be bottled for use.

GOOSEBERRY WINE

Firm green	2 pt cold water to
gooseberries	each lb of fruit

To each gal of juice obtained allow:

3 lb loaf sugar	$\frac{3}{4}$ oz isinglass
$\frac{1}{2}$ pt gin	

Top and tail the gooseberries, bruise them thoroughly, pour the cold water over, and let them stand for about 4 days, stirring frequently. Strain through a jelly bag or fine hair or nylon sieve. Dissolve the sugar in the liquid, add the gin, and the isinglass dissolved in a little warm water, and pour into a cask. Bung loosely until fermentation has ceased, then tighten the bung, and let the cask remain undisturbed for at least 6 months. At the end of this time the wine may be bottled, but it will not be ready for use for at least 12 months.

GRAPE WINE

Sound, not over-ripe grapes	1 qt cold water to each lb of fruit

To each gal of liquid obtained allow:

3 lb loaf sugar	¼ pt brandy
¼ oz isinglass (approx)	

Strip the grapes from the stalks, put them into a wooden tub or earthenware bowl, and bruise them well with a wooden mallet or spoon. Pour over them the water, let them stand for 3 days, stirring frequently, then strain through a jelly bag, or fine hair or nylon sieve. Dissolve the sugar in the liquid, then pour into a cask. Bung lightly for a few days until fermentation subsides, then add the isinglass dissolved in a little warm water, and the brandy, and tighten the bung. Let the cask remain undisturbed for 6 months, then rack the wine off into bottles, cork and seal securely. Keep for at least a year before using.
Note: If the grapes are very sweet the sugar may be omitted.

LEMON WINE

10 lemons	4 qt boiling water
4 lb loaf sugar	Dried yeast

Remove the rinds of 5 lemons in thin fine strips, and place in a wooden tub or earthenware bowl. Boil the sugar and water together for ½ hr, then pour the syrup over the lemon peel. When cool add the strained juice of the 10 lemons, add the yeast, and let the vessel stand for 48 hr. Then strain into a cask,

which the wine must quite fill, bung loosely until fermentation ceases, then tighten the bung, and allow the cask to remain undisturbed for about 6 months before racking the wine off into bottles.

MEAD

2 egg whites	½ in cinnamon stick
3 gal water	3 cloves
5 lb honey	½ in whole ginger
1 blade of mace	Dried yeast

Beat the egg whites slightly, put into a large pan with the water, honey, mace, cinnamon, cloves and ginger. Whisk or stir frequently till boiling-point is reached, then simmer gently for 1 hr. Allow to cool, strain into a cask, add the yeast, cover the bung-hole with a folded cloth until fermentation ceases, then bung tightly, and let the cask stand in a cool, dry place for 9 months. Then rack the mead carefully into bottles, and cork them tightly. The mead may be used at once, but it will keep good for years if stored in a cool, dry place.

MEAD WINE

5 lb honey	2 oz dried hops
5 gal water	Yeast

Dissolve the honey in the water, add the hops, and simmer very gently for 1 hr; turn into an earthenware bowl, let it become lukewarm, then add the yeast. Allow it to remain covered for 3 days, then strain the liquid into a cask, bung loosely until fermentation subsides, and afterwards tighten the bung. The wine should remain in the cask for 12 months, and then be racked off carefully into bottles.

PARSNIP WINE

4 lb parsnips	3 lb demerara sugar
4 qt boiling water	Dried yeast
¼ oz mild hops	spread on toast

Boil the parsnips gently in the water for

15 min, add the hops, and cook for 10 min longer. Strain, add the sugar, let the liquid become lukewarm and put in the toast spread with the yeast. Let it ferment for 36 hr, then turn into a cask, which it should fill. As soon as fermentation ceases, strain into bottles, cork lightly at first, and store in a cool, dry place for at least 1 month before using.

PEACH WINE

12 lb sound, ripe peaches	2 oranges
6½ lb loaf sugar	1 lemon
2½ gal water	1 pt brandy
3 small eggs	½ oz gelatine
A little yeast	½ oz candy sugar

Cut the peaches into slices and place in a large bowl with 2½ lb crushed sugar sprinkled over. Let them remain undisturbed for at least 24 hr. Boil the water and stir in 4 lb sugar and the stiffly whisked egg whites and cook for 20 min, removing the scum as it rises. Add the peaches and sugar and continue to boil until the fruit is reduced to a pulp, removing the scum as it rises. Remove the peach stones and crush them. Put them into a large bowl or tub and pour over the hot fruit pulp. Let the bowl or tub stand until the contents are lukewarm, then add the yeast. Cover with a clean cloth and let it remain undisturbed for 3–4 days. Strain through a sieve and pour into a clean cask, keeping back about 1 qt of the liquid to fill up the cask as fermentation subsides. Add the strained juice and thinly peeled rinds of the oranges and lemon. As soon as the hissing has ceased, pour in the brandy and secure the bung. Let the cask stand for 2 months, then rack the wine off and filter the lees. Pour the wine back into the cask together with the dissolved gelatine and candy sugar. Secure the bung and leave the cask undisturbed for at least 6 months. The wine may then be bottled and the corks sealed; it should be kept at least for another 6 months before it is used.

Nectarine Wine: As above, substituting nectarines for peaches.

Plum Wine: Substitute plums for peaches. The weight of plums to the gallon is an individual matter, for by increasing the plums this wine can be made to resemble a port. Put the plums in the fermenting vessel and pour over them the proportionate amount of boiling water. Then squeeze and stir the pulp daily for about 6 days, and follow instructions above.

RAISIN WINE

Raisins
To each lb raisins allow:

1 gal cold water	Dried yeast
2 lb preserving sugar	

Strip the raisins from the stalks, put the raisins into a large boiler or clean copper pan with the water, simmer gently for about 1 hr, then rub them through a sieve. Dissolve the sugar in the liquid, and add the raisin pulp and the yeast, let the vessel stand covered for 3 days, then strain the liquid into a cask. Bung loosely until fermentation ceases, then tighten the bung, and allow the cask to stand for at least 12 months before racking the wine off into bottles.

RASPBERRY WINE

10 qt ripe rasp- berries
10 qt boiling water
6 lb preserving sugar
1 pt brandy
¼ oz isinglass

Put the prepared fruit into an earthenware or wooden vessel, pour the boiling water over, and let it remain covered until the following day. Pass both liquid and fruit through a fine hair or nylon sieve, let it stand for 24 hr, then strain it carefully into another vessel, without disturbing the sediment. Add the sugar, and as soon as it is dissolved, turn into a clean, dry cask. Cover the bung-hole with a folded cloth until fermentation subsides, then bung it closely. Let it stand for 1 month, rack it off into a clean cask, add the brandy and isinglass dissolved in a little warm water, bung tightly, and allow it to remain undisturbed for 12 months. Then rack it off into bottles, cork securely, store for 12 months longer, and the wine will be ready for use.

REDCURRANT WINE

1 gal ripe red-currants	5 lb loaf OR preserving sugar
1½ gal cold water	½ pt brandy

Remove the stalks from the currants, put the currants into an earthenware bowl, bruise them well with a wooden spoon, and drain off the juice. Put the juice aside, add the water to the berries, let it stand for 2–3 hr, stirring occasionally meanwhile. At the end of this time strain the liquid from the berries into the juice, add three-quarters of the sugar, stir occasionally until dissolved, then pour into a cask, filling it three-quarters full. Bung closely, but place a vent peg in the bung of the cask, and let the cask remain for 1 month. Dissolve the remainder of the sugar in the smallest possible quantity of warm water, mix it well with the contents of the cask, replace the bung, and allow the cask to remain undisturbed for 6 weeks longer. Drain off the wine into a clean, dry cask, add the brandy, let the cask stand for about 6 months in a dry, warm place, then bottle and cork tightly.

The wine may be used at once, but will be better if kept for 12 months at least.

RHUBARB WINE

25 lb rhubarb	1 oz isinglass
5 gal cold water	

To each gal of liquid obtained allow:

3 lb loaf OR preserving sugar	1 lemon

Wipe the rhubarb with a damp cloth, and cut it into short lengths, without skinning it. Put into an earthenware or wooden vessel, crush it thoroughly with a wooden mallet or other heavy instrument, and pour over it the water. Let it remain covered for 10 days, stirring daily; then strain the liquor into another vessel, add the sugar, lemon juice and rind in the proportions given above, and stir occasionally until the sugar is dissolved.

Then put it into a cask, and add the isinglass previously dissolved in a little warm water; cover the bung-hole with a folded cloth for 10 days, then bung securely, and allow it to remain undisturbed for 12 months. Rack off into bottles and use.

ROWAN WINE

4 gal sound, ripe rowanberries	1 oz isinglass and 1 pt brandy to each gal of wine
Boiling water	
Loaf sugar	

The berries should be gathered on a fine, dry day. Bruise them well and place them in a tub. Just cover with boiling water. Cover the tub with a clean cloth and let it stand undisturbed for 3 days. Carefully remove the scum and strain the liquid through a sieve into a large basin, measuring it carefully. To every gallon of liquid allow 1 lb crushed loaf sugar. Stir until it is thoroughly dissolved, then pour the wine into a clean cask, keeping back a quart or so to fill up the cask as fermentation subsides. As soon as the hissing has entirely ceased, pour in the dissolved isinglass and brandy. Secure the bung. The wine will be ready to bottle at the end of 6 months.

SLOE WINE

4 gal sound, ripe sloes	$\frac{1}{2}$ oz isinglass and 1 qt brandy to every 3 gal wine
4 gal boiling water	
4 lb loaf sugar to every gal of liquid	

Crush the fruit and put it into a tub with the boiling water. Let it stand for 5 days, stirring from time to time. Strain off the liquid and measure it. Add sugar in the proportion stated above and stir until it is dissolved. Pour the liquid into a clean cask, reserving a quart or so to fill up with as fermentation dies down. Keep the cask filled up and as soon as the hissing ceases, pour in the brandy and dissolved isinglass. Secure the bung and bottle at the end of 2 years or less if the wine seems clear.

SLOE GIN

Sloes	Noyeau OR almond essence
Barley sugar	Gin

Half-fill clean, dry wine bottles with the fruit previously pricked with a darning needle. Add to each 1 oz crushed barley sugar, a little noyeau, or 2–3 drops of almond essence. Fill the bottles with unsweetened gin, cork securely, and allow to remain in a moderately warm place for 3 months. Then strain the liqueur through fine muslin or filter paper until quite clear. Bottle, cork securely and store for use.

Note: Although not really a wine this recipe has been included in response to many requests.

TURNIP WINE

Turnips	Loaf sugar

To every gal of juice obtained allow:

3 lb loaf sugar	$\frac{1}{2}$ pt brandy

Wash, peel and slice the turnips thinly, sprinkle over them a little crushed sugar and let them remain until next day. Pound and squeeze out as much juice as possible, measure and pour it into a clean cask. Add sugar and brandy in the proportion stated above. Keep the cask filled up while the wine is working and as soon as fermentation has ceased secure the bung. The wine will be ready for bottling at the end of 3 months. It should be kept for another 12 months before use.

HOME-BREWED BEERS

BIRCH BEER

$\frac{1}{2}$ lb black birch bark	$\frac{1}{4}$ lb ginger
1 oz hops	6 pt golden syrup
$\frac{1}{4}$ lb pimento	$\frac{1}{2}$ pt yeast

Boil the bark in 3–4 pt water and, when considerably reduced, strain and boil rapidly until the liquor is as thick as treacle. Meanwhile boil the hops, pimento and ginger in 6 qt water for 20 min, then strain it on to the bark extract. Stir until it boils, add the golden syrup and when quite dissolved, strain into a cask. Add 10 gallons water previously boiled and allowed to cool, and as soon as it becomes lukewarm stir in the liquid yeast. Let it remain loosely bunged for 2–3 days, or until fermentation has ceased, then strain into small bottles, cork them tightly, and store in a cool place.

GINGER BEER

2 lemons	5 qt boiling water
1¼ lb sugar	1 good tablesp
1 oz whole ginger	fresh yeast
¼ oz cream of tartar	

Remove the rinds of the lemons as thinly as possible, strip off every particle of white pith, slice the lemons thinly, removing the pips. Put the slices into an earthenware bowl with the sugar, ginger and cream of tartar, and pour in the boiling water. Allow it to stand until lukewarm, then stir in the yeast and let the bowl remain in a moderately warm place for 24 hr. Skim off the yeast, strain the ginger beer carefully from the sediment, bottle, tie the corks down securely. It will be ready in 2 days.

HOP BEER

5 oz hops	2½ lb brown sugar
8 gal water	3–4 tablesp yeast

Boil the hops and water together for 45 min, add the sugar and, when dissolved, strain into a bowl or tub. As soon as it is lukewarm add the yeast, let it work for 48 hr, then skim well, and strain into bottles, or a small cask. Cork securely, and let it remain for a few days before using.

NETTLE BEER

½ peck young nettle tops	12 oz loaf sugar
2 lb malt	1 oz hops
1 gal water	A little yeast on
2 oz sarsaparilla	toast

Boil the nettle tops and the malt in the water for ½ hr, then stir in the sarsaparilla, loaf sugar and hops. Stand aside to cool and when just lukewarm, add the yeast. Let stand for a while but bottle off while still working.

Candied Fruits and Flowers

SHOP-BOUGHT CANDIED fruits are expensive luxuries. One can save a good deal by making them at home from fresh fruit, purchased when it is in season at its cheapest. Most years there are, for example, cheap, well-flavoured fresh pineapples and small peaches.

Scarcely any skill is needed to produce professional-looking results. But you do need patience; you will have to spend a few minutes looking after the fruit practically every day for several days. Impatient attempts to speed-up the process only shrivels and toughens the fruit. The water in the fruit must diffuse out slowly; it must be replaced gradually by a syrup which is steadily increased in strength. In this way, the fruit is slowly impregnated with sugar but remains plump and tender.

The method is given in detail below.

HOW TO CANDY FRESH FRUITS

1 Choose well flavoured firm-ripe fruit, not too ripe. Peaches or pears should be peeled and stoned or cored and cut into quarters, cherries should be stoned; pineapples should be peeled and cut into slices, then into wedge-shaped pieces; small crabapples, apricots and fleshy plums and greengages should be pricked several times to the centre with a stainless fork. For angelica and orange, grapefruit and lemon peel, see recipes for special preparations.

2 Cover the prepared fruit with boiling water and simmer gently until just tender when tested with a fine skewer (about 10–15 min for firm

fruits; only 3–4 min for tender fruits). Test frequently because over-cooking at this stage would make the fruit squashy, whilst under-cooking would make it dark and tough.

3 For each 1 lb of fruit make a syrup from $\frac{1}{2}$ pt of the water in which the fruit was cooked, plus 2 oz sugar, plus 4 oz glucose. Alternatively, use $\frac{1}{2}$ pt of the water, plus 6 oz granulated or preserving sugar. Stir until the sugar is dissolved, then bring to the boil.

4 Pour the boiling syrup over the drained fruit which has been placed in a small bowl. If there is not sufficient syrup to cover it, make up some more using the same proportion of sweetening to water. Leave the fruit in the syrup for 24 hr, keeping it below the surface with a plate or saucer.

5 2nd Day: Drain off the syrup into a saucepan, add 2 oz sugar for each original $\frac{1}{2}$ pt (i.e. add 4 oz if you originally made up 1 pt of syrup), bring to the boil and pour again over the fruit in the bowl.

6 3rd Day: Repeat step 5.

7 4th Day: Repeat step 5.

8 5th Day: Repeat step 5.

9 6th Day: Now add 3 oz of sugar for every original $\frac{1}{2}$ pt, heat and stir to dissolve in the saucepan. Add the drained fruit and boil for 3–4 min before pouring it all back into the bowl. (Boiling the fruit in the syrup in these final stages helps to make it plump.) Leave for 48 hr.

10 8th Day: Repeat step 9. When the resulting syrup cools, it should then be of the consistency of a fairly thick honey. Leave for 4 days. If the syrup is still thin when it cools on the 8th day, repeat step 9 again before leaving to soak for the 4 days.

11 At last the process is nearly complete. You may take a holiday from it at this stage because it will keep in this heavy syrup for 2–3 weeks. But if you are anxious to progress, remove the fruit from the syrup—using a fork—after the 4 days. Place the fruit on a wire cake rack with a plate beneath to catch the drainings. Allow the syrup to drain for a few minutes.

12 Put the rack into a very cool oven (not more

than 50 °C, 120 °F) i.e. with an electric cooker use residual heat after cooking, with gas, if the thermostat and tap are separate, set the thermostat at the highest mark, then turn down the gas to a glimmer with the tap. If the thermostat and tap are in one, turn to the lowest glimmer. On some cookers there is a very cool control which can be used. Drying off should take 3–6 hr if the heat is continuous; it may take 2–3 days if you use residual heat on several occasions. Turn the fruit gently with a fork, until it is no longer sticky to handle. In summer, the fruit can be dried by putting it in the sunshine for a few hours.

13 Pack in cardboard boxes with waxed paper lining the box and separating the layers. If properly stored, candied fruits should keep for many months.

Note: Only one variety of fruit should be candied in the syrup; if you are candying several fruits, at the same time, use separate syrups. Do not waste the surplus syrup—use it for fruit salads or stewed fruit, or for sweetening puddings. Alternatively, let it take the place of sugar in fruit chutneys.

Candied fresh fruit chart

Day	Amount sweetening per ½ pt	Method	Leave soaking for:
1st	2 oz sugar 4 oz glucose OR 6 oz sugar	Dissolve sugar. Bring syrup to boiling-point. Pour over the drained cooked fruit.	24 hr 24 hr
2nd	2 oz sugar		24 hr
3rd	2 oz sugar		24 hr
4th	2 oz sugar		24 hr
5th	2 oz sugar		24 hr
6th	3 oz sugar	Dissolve sugar, add fruit, boil in the syrup for 3–4 min. Then return all to the bowl.	48 hr
8th	3 oz sugar	As above. Repeat, if necessary, so that the syrup when cold, is the consistency of a fairly thick honey.	4 days
12th	nil	Dry in a very cool oven—not exceeding 50 °C, 120 °F. Or dry in the sunshine.	

CANDIED ANGELICA
Pick the stalks in April, when they are tender and brightly coloured. Cut off the root ends and leaves. Make a brine from $\frac{1}{4}$ oz salt to 2 qt water, bring it to the boil and cover the stalks with it. Leave to soak for 10 min. Rinse in cold water. Put in a pan of fresh boiling water and boil for 5–7 min. Drain. Scrape to remove the outer skin.
Continue as for the method 'To Candy Fresh Fruits'.

CANDIED PEEL
Use oranges, lemons or grapefruit, and wash the fruit thoroughly, scrubbing with a clean brush if necessary. Cut in halves, carefully removing the pulp to avoid damaging the peel. Boil the peel for 1 hr. Give grapefruit peel, which is bitter, several changes of water. Drain and continue as for 'To Candy Fresh Fruits'.

CANDIED PEEL (quick method)
Use oranges, grapefruit or lemons, but soak peel from grapefruit or lemons overnight to extract some of its bitterness. Cut the peel into long strips $\frac{1}{4}$ in wide. Put in a saucepan, cover with cold water and bring slowly to the boil. Drain off the water. Add fresh water and bring to the boil, as before. Drain and repeat 3 times, making 5 boilings altogether. Weigh the cooled peel and weigh an equal quantity of sugar. Place the peel and sugar in a pan and just cover with boiling water. Boil gently until peel is tender and clear. Cool, strain from the syrup and toss the peel in fine granulated sugar on greaseproof paper. Spread out on a wire rack to dry for several hours. Roll again in sugar if at all sticky. When quite dry, store in covered jars.
Note: This method is useful if the peel is not to be kept longer than 3–4 months.

To give a glacé finish to candied fruit
This is a more professional finish—it coats the fruit with a smooth, shiny glaze—but it calls for a special piece of equipment, an hydrometer. This tool can be used both for the candying and the glacé finish. It may be worth buying by the house-

wife who intends to candy large quantities of fruit, but it is not essential for candying, so the method of doing that is not given in detail here. But if you wish to use an hydrometer for a *glacé* finish, here is the method:

Make a fresh syrup by dissolving 1 lb sugar in $\frac{1}{4}$ pt water, to give a syrup of 65 °Brix at 38 °C, 100 °F. Bring to boil. Lift each piece of candied fruit on a candying fork or skewer and dip it in boiling water for 20 seconds. Drain on a wire tray. Half-fill a hot cup or small basin with boiling syrup and quickly dip the fruit in and out. Drain on a wire tray. Use fresh syrup (kept hot in the tightly covered pan) as soon as the first portion becomes cloudy. Put in a warm place—not more than 50 °C, 120 °F—to dry, turning the fruit occasionally. Pack as for candied fruits.

HOW TO CANDY FLOWERS

You can candy flowers by cooking them in a sugar and water syrup until the syrup begins to granulate. Small rosebuds, violets, and the yellow 'pips' of cowslips are particularly suitable for this treatment.

The flowers should be gathered early when the dew has just dried. Bring 4 fluid oz water to the boil and stir in 8 oz granulated sugar until dissolved. Remove any stems from flowers, and lightly wash and drain them without bruising. Heat the syrup and stir in the flowers and cook gently to 130 °C, 250 °F (soft ball stage). Take off the heat and stir until the syrup begins to granulate to the texture of coarse meal. Pour into a colander and shake off the extra sugar as the flowers cool. Store in jars with the lids sealed with sticky tape. This quantity of syrup will be enough for 1 breakfastcup of small rosebuds, or 2 breakfastcups of violets.

CRYSTALLIZED FOR GLITTER!
Crystallizing flowers

Many types of flowers can be crystallized to use as cake decorations or small sweets, and they will last several months and keep their natural colours. Primroses, violets, polyanthus, roses, carnation petals, forget-me-nots, mimosa, cowslips, sweet peas and fruit blossoms are suitable for crystallizing. Flowers which come from bulbs should not be eaten.

CRYSTALLIZED FLOWERS

The flowers may be crystallized in a solution of gum Arabic crystals and rose or orangeflower water. Allow 3 teasp crystals to 3 tablsp rosewater, and leave in a screwtop jar for 2 or 3 days, shaking occasionally until the mixture is a sticky glue. Use a small soft paintbrush to paint the flowers, coating them completely, or bare spots will shrivel and not keep. Large flowers must be taken apart and the petals reassembled when needed. The flowers should then be tossed lightly in castor sugar and left in a cool place for about 24 hr until crisp and dry. It is best to store these in a dark place, preferably in a tin sealed with sticky tape.

CRYSTALLIZED FLOWERS (short-keeping)

Fresh mint leaves, or rose or carnation petals
Egg white
Granulated sugar
Use very fresh leaves or petals which are well shaped. Beat the egg white stiffly and coat both sides of the leaves. Coat with sugar and put on a wire rack covered with waxed paper. Put on the rack of a cooker until crisp and dry. Keep in a tin between layers of waxed paper. These will not keep long, but are nice to use for garnishing ice cream or cold puddings.

A CRYSTALLIZINE FINISH FOR CANDIED FRUITS

Dip one piece of candied fruit quickly into boiling water. Drain off excess water. Roll the piece of fruit in fine granulated or castor sugar, which has been spread out on clean paper. Repeat the process with the other pieces of candied fruit and allow to dry in the air.

Freezing for Freshness

QUICK FREEZING is becoming an increasingly popular way of preserving foods.

Most refrigerators now have an ice-making compartment big enough for short-term storage of a fair amount of frozen food. Many compartments are marked with one, two or three stars, indicating how long foods can be stored safely (i.e. how low the interior temperature of the compartment is). But none is cold enough for quick-freezing unfrozen foods safely. For this, one needs a special freezer unit which can have an interior temperature of between minus 17 °C, 0 °F, and minus 12 °C, 10 °F, or colder. (Real 'deep freezing' is only possible commercially; commercial frozen-food stores are kept at about minus 30–35 °C, minus 22–31 °F.)

A refrigerator is, however, a vital adjunct to a freezer, since foods can be chilled in it before freezing, and most foods are better if thawed slowly at refrigerator temperature (1–10 °C or 35–50 °F).

Careful use of a freezer will fairly soon offset the capital outlay on the machine. Large quantities of home-grown and reared products can be preserved, at their prime, in glut periods. Moreover, when cooking meals 'make two and freeze one' saves time, labour and fuel, and prevents wastage of ingredients and money.

In addition to freezing poultry, meat, fruit and vegetables, many small quantities or portions of cooked food can be frozen and kept in the freezer until required. For instance, game or poultry, especially turkey, can be enjoyed so much more in smaller amounts at more frequent intervals.

Even small quantities of stock or soup which are not required for immediate consumption can be safely stored in the freezer until required. Such things as sponge cakes, genoese pastries (decorated with butter cream) mince pies, etc, can be prepared in readiness for Christmas three or four weeks ahead if necessary, which can be a great convenience. Larger quantities of yeast breads and rolls may be mixed up at one time and some of the unbaked doughs may be frozen for as long as two weeks. Freshly baked breads may be wrapped and frozen as soon as they are cool. This will keep them fresh for two or three weeks.

Besides home-grown and home-made products, a freezer keeps ready for use the whole range of frozen foods which can now be purchased in bags or packets. Some of these contain single ingredients, such as peas. Sometimes mixed vegetables or fruits are packaged. Pastry is available, both in slab form and as ready-cut vols-au-vent or tartlets. Made-up dishes can also be bought, which only need brief cooking or re-heating; some of the better ones come in linked 'boil-in-the-bag' packs, one holding a starchy vegetable, the other a meat or fish mixture.

There is no need to use a whole packet or bag of many frozen goods at one time. If vegetables or fruits are bought in loose packs, a suitable quantity can be shaken out for use, and the bag can be re-fastened and re-stored. The same applies to goods like hamburgers, fish fillets and vol-au-vent cases.

Choice of food

Many fruits and vegetables freeze very well. But all should be nearly ripe, firm, in good condition and freshly picked. Freezing cannot improve poor food. Try to freeze produce as soon as it is picked or bought, but if this is not possible, keep it in a cool place, preferably a refrigerator not longer than 24 hr.

Choice of containers

All foods to be frozen must be suitably wrapped or

Selection of food for a freezer.

packed to avoid drying out in the freezer. If even-sized containers are carefully stacked, it is often possible to pack about 20 lb of solid food into 1 cubic foot of storage space. Make up packages of a size most suitable to serve for one meal; this avoids leftover defrosted food. Food must not be re-frozen once it has thawed.

If possible, choose square or rectangular cartons rather than irregular-shaped containers which take up more space. They must be airtight. Wrapping materials must be moisture-vapour-proof, and greaseproof. Large articles such as chicken, turkeys, joints, etc can be over-wrapped with mutton cloth or paper after they have been sealed. This is to protect the container from being torn by another package in the freezer. Wax tubs, rigid containers, polythene bags, low-temperature resistant glass jars without shoulders, aluminium foil and self-stick transparent wrapping can all be

Blanching cauliflower for freezing.

used if properly tied or sealed. The air inside must be pressed out as far as possible, and all projecting edges on the food should be wrapped up, before sealing.

Label all packages with a felt pen marker and keep a list of the goods stored.

Fruits may be frozen, unsweetened. But for the best flavour, colour and texture, it is advisable to freeze them with granulated sugar *or* cover them with a syrup. Glut garden crops are useful frozen for jam-making later.

Syrup Prepare this in advance and use when quite cold. It can be stored for a week or so in a refrigerator.

The amount of sugar used can be varied according to taste. The recommended strengths are:

2 oz sugar dissolved in water and made up to
1 pt = 10%

4 oz sugar dissolved in water and made up to
1 pt = 20%

6 oz sugar dissolved in water and made up to
1 pt = 30%

8 oz sugar dissolved in water and made up to
1 pt = 40%

10 oz sugar dissolved in water and made up to
1 pt = 50%.
Method: Bring the sugar and water just to the
boil. Cover to prevent evaporation and put to one
side until quite cold. Allow about 1 pt of syrup
to each 2 lb fruit. This should be sufficient to
cover the fruit.

Freezing vegetables

In order to keep the colour, flavour and food
value during storage, it is essential to blanch
vegetables before packing and freezing.
To blanch Do not blanch more than 1–2 lb of
vegetables at a time. After preparing the vegetables, bring some water to a rolling boil in a large
saucepan (allow 8 pt of water for 1–2 lb of non-
leafy vegetables; for leafy vegetables, allow 12 pt
of water).
Place the vegetables in a wire basket or in a muslin
bag. Immerse them in the boiling water, note the
time, and bring the water rapidly to the boil
again. Move the vegetables around in the water
for the time given in the table below. Remove
immediately the time is up, and chill thoroughly
in ice-cold water. Drain, pack into a moisture-
vapour-proof container and seal. A moisture-
vapour-proof bag is an easy container to use in
freezing vegetables.
The same water may be used for successive batches
of the same vegetable. Do not add any salt to the
water. Salt should not be added until the frozen
vegetables are removed from their packets for
cooking.

Filling containers with fruits or vegetables

1 Just as water expands when turning into ice, so
fruit purée or fruit in syrup expand when frozen.
Therefore the container should never be com-
pletely filled. Leave $\frac{1}{2}$–$\frac{3}{4}$ in head space, according
to the size of the carton.
2 If the fruit is packed plain or in dry sugar, there
is no need to leave space. It is the water which
expands, not the fruit.

3 Vegetables are packed without added liquid, so they can come almost to the brim of the container, or can be wrapped tightly in suitable material.

4 Avoid wetting the seal edges of packets. A wide-mouthed funnel is useful for filling neatly.

Freezing poultry

Choose only the best-quality, healthy, well-formed birds for quick freezing. Clean and wash well in running water, and drain.

For freezing, truss the bird as for the table. Wrap the well-washed giblets in greaseproof paper, moisture-proof cellophane or plastic material and place by the side of the bird.

Package the bird in a moisture-vapour-proof container, a bag being the most suitable for quick handling. If the bones of the legs are sharp and pointed, wrap small pieces of foil round them so that they do not pierce the bag. Label, mark weight of bird and date frozen.

The bag should now be carefully sealed either by heat-sealing or with a bag fastener, or with special sealing tape; see below.

Jointed birds Wrap each piece separately in greaseproof paper, moisture-proof cellophane, or polythene, in either a waxed carton, a moisture-proof bag or fibre tray.

Giblets are wrapped in the same way.

Freezing meat

Choose only good-quality meat for freezing. Protect all cuts from loss of moisture during the freezing and storing process by proper packaging. When preparing roasting joints, etc, each piece of meat must be wrapped individually, eliminating as much air as possible from the package by pressing and wrapping material close to the meat. Meat can be wrapped in a variety of ways; the easiest is to use a bag which can be filled, sealed by heat or with a bag fastener or special sealing tape. When emptied it can be washed thoroughly and put away for future use.

When preparing chops, fillets, etc, first trim off excess fat. When packing two or more pieces of meat in one container, the portions should be separated by placing two small pieces of greaseproof paper or cellophane between them. (By doing this it is quite easy to take out any piece of meat while still solidly frozen.) The meat should then be packed in a suitable container for quick freezing and storing.

Each package should be marked with the date, weight of the meat or any other remarks required. When meat is packed in polythene bags or sheets of moisture-vapour-proof materials, it is wise to overwrap it with strong paper or mutton cloth.

Baked and dairy goods

Most baked goods freeze extremely well. Dairy produce is less successful. Cream should be pasteurized and cooled rapidly and contain 40 per cent butter fat; if it has a lower content it tends to separate. Milk may curdle. Hard cheeses can freeze well, but softer cheeses may crumble. It is inadvisable to freeze cakes with fillings as these tend to go soggy. So does meringue. Gelatine goes cloudy, but is fine for opaque dishes.

Many ready-prepared desserts (including, obviously, ice creams) freeze well, and a selection of recipes for making them and freezing them is given in this book.

Sealing

Special waxed containers should be sealed with adhesive tape sold for this purpose. Tubs have lids which seal into a groove, or screw tops.

When using bags made of moisture-vapour-proof materials they need to be heat-sealed with a warm iron, curling tongs or a bag fastener; squeeze out as much air as possible before sealing. Some materials need to be protected from direct contact with the iron by a piece of paper.

Before wrapping meat, poultry or game, cover all sharp ends of bone with several thicknesses of clean kitchen paper, to avoid piercing the wrapper.

Labelling and stacking

Do not attempt to use ordinary stick-on labels in the freezer, or to write in ink. Mark the container with a chinagraph pencil or felt pen. Note the variety, quantity and the amount of sugar or syrup (if used) and the date, e.g. 'Whole strawberries, 15 oz; in 40% syrup; July 20, 19—'.

PACKING FOR THE FREEZER

Chicken

Beef

Vegetables

Fruit

Stack the containers closely (once food is frozen, the closer it is stacked the better. It is in the freezing process that they must not touch). Tubs are most economically stacked with every other one upside down. Do not over-load the freezer at the actual time of freezing fresh produce. Freezer manufacturers issue pamphlets stating the maximum freezing load.

Storage

1 Once frozen, it is a good idea to keep similar varieties together, either with coloured paper or tapes, or in string nets, or cardboard boxes or special baskets provided with some freezers. (These can be purchased separately and used in other models.) Keep a plan showing where the produce is stored—this saves keeping the freezer open while you search for a particular packet.

2 It is best not to store frozen food for longer than a year. Plan to have a quick turnover of stock, with as much variety as possible.

3 If there is a short power cut, do not open the cabinet unless it is really necessary. It should remain at a temperature sufficiently low not to harm the food. Food kept like this should be all right for 12–36 hours, depending on the type, size and the insulation of the freezer. If you are moving house and the freezer has to be emptied, pack the food with dry newspaper for transport.

4 To defrost, follow the manufacturers' instructions carefully. With careful handling defrosting will probably only be necessary about once a year. But do not leave it too long because too much ice round the inside of the compartment takes up space and impairs the efficiency of the freezer.

To use frozen foods

Fruits To preserve the best appearance allow fruit to thaw gradually when required for dessert use. Do not open the packet while the food is thawing; merely leave it at room temperature for 3–4 hr per 1 lb weight, or leave it (still unopened) in a domestic refrigerator for 5–6 hr per 1 lb weight.

If you are in a hurry for the fruit, place an unopened pack in cold water allowing the tap to run slightly, so changing the water.

Fruit to be used for cooking need not be defrosted first.

Vegetables Corn on the cob should be thawed before it is cooked, or the outside will be overcooked before the heat can penetrate properly to the inside.

It is unnecessary to thaw any other deep-frozen vegetables before cooking. As a general rule, allow about $\frac{1}{2}$ pt water and $\frac{1}{2}$ teasp salt to a 1 lb pack, adding any other seasoning to taste. Bring the salted water to the boil, add the frozen vegetables, and as they heat, break up the block with a fork to help it to thaw quickly. Boil for only about $\frac{1}{2}$ the time needed to cook fresh vegetables. Cooking time is counted from the time the water begins to boil again.

Meat or poultry Joints of meat or poultry must be fully thawed before cooking. Allow 5–6 hr per lb if thawed in a domestic refrigerator or 2–3 hr per lb if thawed at room temperature. If more rapid thawing is necessary, place the sealed package in a warm place or in the draught from an electric fan, allowing about 45 min per lb in weight. The meat should be left in the unopened package while thawing. Cook the food as soon as possible after it has been completely thawed, as at this stage it keeps less well than fresh food; once it has been cooked, however, it will keep for the same time as similarly cooked fresh meat.

Chops, sausages and thin portions of meat can be cooked without thawing, but will take longer to cook than usual.

FRUIT AND VEGETABLE CHART

Fruit	Method of Preparation	Type of pack
Apple slices (good cooking variety)	Peel, core and slice. Scald or blanch for 3 min. (Work quickly to prevent discoloration. If cutting up large quantities, scald them in batches.)	Pack plain or cover completely with 20% syrup.
Apple purée (good cooking variety)	Stew, then rub through a sieve.	Mix 1 lb granulated sugar with 4–5 lb pulped apple, or freeze without sugar.
Apricots	Wash, cut in halves, stone, peel.	Cover with 40% syrup.*
Blackberries	Sort and stem. If really necessary, rinse gently in ice-cold water and drain well.	Pack plain (sugar can be added at the cooking stage) or cover with 50% syrup or mix I lb granulated sugar with 3–4 lb fruit.
Blackberry and Apple	Clean the blackberries. Peel, core and slice the apples, working quickly to avoid browning. Mix in required quantities.	Mix 1 lb granulated sugar with 4–5 lb fruit.
Cherries (a well-flavoured black variety)	Stem. Rinse gently in ice-cold water. Stone if desired.	Cover with 30% syrup.
Currants (black or red)	Stem. If really necessary, rinse gently in ice-cold water and drain well.	Cover with 30% syrup. or mix 1 lb granulated sugar with 3 lb currants.
Gooseberries	Pick just before fully ripened. Top and tail. Wash in ice-cold water. Drain.	Pack plain if for cooking, or with sugar if desired.
Grapes (delicate flavour, tender skins)	Stem. Wash in ice-cold water. Drain. Cut in half and take the pips out. Grapes need careful defrosting.	Cover with 30% syrup.

Fruit	Preparation	To freeze
Grapefruit, oranges, tangerines	Chill. Wash, peel and remove all pith. Remove segments by cutting along membrane (or halve and remove the fruit pulp with a grapefruit spoon). Remove pips. (Work quickly, preparing one or two packages at a time.)	Pack in own juice without sugar or mix 1 part granulated sugar with 4 parts fruit segments by weight or cover with 50% syrup for grapefruit and 30% for oranges.
Juice of grapefruit, oranges, tangerines, lemons	Extract the juice and strain it through a double thickness of muslin. Fill into the containers to within $\frac{1}{2}$ in of the lid.	Freeze plain, immediately.
Loganberries, raspberries	Look over carefully. Do not wash them unless necessary. If essential, rinse a few at a time in ice-cold water. Drain.	Pack without sugar or cover with 40% syrup or mix 1 lb granulated sugar with 3–4 lb fruit.
Loganberry or raspberry purée	After sorting and rinsing if necessary, rub fruit through a sieve.	Mix 1 part sugar with 4–5 parts sieved fruit.
Peaches	Peel, stone and slice.	Cover with 40% syrup.*
Plums (dark variety)	Stem. Rinse in ice-cold water. Drain.	Cover with 40% syrup.
Rhubarb	Wash, trim and cut stalks into 1 in lengths.	Pack plain or cover with 30% syrup or mix 1 lb granulated sugar with 5 lb rhubarb.
Strawberries (firm, ripe, well-coloured)	Remove calyx. Rinse a few at a time in ice-cold water. Drain. Slice or leave whole. Weigh.	Mix 1 lb granulated sugar with 4–5 lb fruit or cover with 40% syrup. Best unsweetened as they are apt to go pulpy.
Strawberry purée	Remove calyx. See Loganberry, raspberry purée.	

* To help preserve the natural colour, slice apricots and peaches into a citric acid solution ($\frac{1}{4}$ teasp citric acid dissolved in 1 qt water. Leave 1–2 min, drain and pack with syrup). Or add $\frac{1}{4}$ teasp ascorbic acid to each teacup of syrup before pouring it over the sliced fruit.

FRUIT AND VEGETABLE CHART

Vegetable	Method of Preparation	Scalding Time
Asparagus	Grade into thick and thin stems. Wash, scrape off bracts, cut so that stems measure 6 in from the tips.	Thin stems: 2 min Thick stems: 4 min
Broad beans (young, **tender)**	Remove pods.	$1\frac{1}{2}$ min
Beans—French or Runner (small, tender)	Wash, top and tail, string if necessary. Leave small beans whole; slice larger ones.	2–3 min
Broccoli, Purple Sprouting	Cut into even lengths, about 2–3 in long. Wash carefully.	4 min
Brussels Sprouts (small, tight 'button' sprouts)	Wash carefully.	4 min
Carrots (young, even sizes)	Wash, scald, then cool and rub off the skins. Leave whole or slice or dice before packing for freezing.	3 min
Cauliflower and Broccoli (Winter Cauliflower)	Break into florets 2 in across.	3 min
Corn-on-the-cob (just mature)	Cut off tough skin, strip off the outer green leaves and the silky threads, and cut off any immature grains. Wash.	Small: 4 min Large: 6 min
Whole grain sweet corn	Prepare as for corn-on-the-cob, cut off the grain with a sharp knife. After scalding and cooling, pack into containers for freezing.	
Peas (good cooking variety, just mature)	Remove pods.	1–2 min
Potatoes (new—avoid potatoes which tend to blacken when cleaned)	Wash, scrape.	4–5 min

Spinach — Wash very thoroughly in several changes of water until free of dirt. Remove tough stems. Divide into batches each weighing about 3 oz. — 2 min

Vegetable Purées (asparagus, beetroot, carrots, parsnips, peas, spinach or turnips) — Cook in boiling water or steam till tender. Mash with a potato ricer so that the purée is smooth without having air whipped into it, or use a kitchen utensil made specially for puréeing foods. Chill, then pack into the container, label and freeze.

A CALENDAR OF GARDEN PRODUCE FOR PRESERVING

JANUARY
Vegetables
Broccoli, Brussels Sprouts, Cabbage, Carrots, Celery, Leeks, Parsnips, Savoy Cabbage, Spinach

Fruit
Apples, Medlars, Pears

FEBRUARY
Vegetables
Artichokes (Jerusalem) Broccoli, Brussels Sprouts, Celery, Leeks, Parsnips, Seakale, Swedes, Savoy Cabbage

Fruit
Apples, Pears

MARCH
Vegetables
Broccoli, Parsnips, Seakale

Fruit
Apples, Rhubarb

APRIL
Vegetables
Parsnips, Seakale, Spinach

Fruit
Apples, Rhubarb

MAY
Vegetables
Asparagus, Cabbage, Cauliflower, New Potatoes, Peas, Seakale, Spinach

Fruit
Apples, Cherries, Gooseberries

JUNE
Vegetables

Asparagus, Broad Beans, French Beans, Cabbage, Carrots, Cauliflower, Peas, Spinach, Turnips, Summer Salads

Fruit

Cherries, Currants, Gooseberries, Raspberries, Strawberries

JULY
Vegetables

Artichokes (Globe), Asparagus, Broad Beans, French Beans, Runner Beans, Carrots, Cauliflower, Peas, Spinach, Turnips, Summer Salads

Fruit

Apricots, Cherries, Currants, Gooseberries, Raspberries, Strawberries

AUGUST
Vegetables

Artichokes (Globe), Asparagus, Cabbage, Carrots, Cauliflower, Marrow, Onions, Peas, Potatoes, Runner Beans, Turnips, Summer Salads

Fruit

Peaches, Plums

SEPTEMBER
Vegetables

Artichokes (Globe), Brussels Sprouts, Cabbage, Carrots, Celery, Marrow, Onions, Peas, Potatoes, Runner Beans, Tomatoes, Turnips

Fruit

Apples, Damsons, Figs, Grapes, Pears, Plums

OCTOBER
Vegetables

Beetroot, Brussels Sprouts, Cabbage, Carrots, Cauliflower, Marrow, Onions, Potatoes, Tomatoes, Turnips

Fruit

Apples, Damsons, Figs, Grapes, Pears, Quinces

NOVEMBER
Vegetables

Beetroot, Brussels Sprouts, Cabbage, Carrots, Celery, Onions, Potatoes, Spinach, Turnips

Fruit

Apples, Grapes, Pears

DECEMBER
Vegetables

Broccoli, Brussels Sprouts, Cabbage, Carrots, Celery, Leeks, Onions, Parsnips, Potatoes, Spinach, Turnips

Fruit

Apples, Pears

Index